AF743397

The European Convention on Human Rights and the COVID-19 Pandemic

This book provides detailed analysis of the applicability of the provisions of the European Convention on Human Rights to issues raised by the COVID-19 pandemic. It encompasses in-depth discussion of the emerging jurisprudence of the European Court of Human Rights relating to issues arising from the pandemic. To date, a substantial number of complaints concerning such issues have been made to the Court. Human rights claims in the context of the pandemic fall into two broad categories: those based on arguments that states did not put in place sufficient measures to protect individuals from the virus and those entailing arguments that the measures put in place themselves involved breaches of rights. The essential question with which the European Court of Human Rights must grapple is how to adjudicate on the correct balance which should have been struck. The book argues that the Court should be cautious of finding breaches of the European Convention on Human Rights in cases involving public restrictions which were applied for the purpose of protecting life and health in response to a global pandemic. If the concept of a human rights violation is defined too broadly, it dilutes the seriousness of such a breach. In particular, it is argued that to preserve the legitimacy of human rights law, the Court must be cautious of applying an overly narrow margin of appreciation in such cases. The work will be of interest to academics, researchers and policymakers working in the area of human rights.

Ronagh J.A. McQuigg is a Reader in the School of Law, Queen's University Belfast. Her research interests are in the area of international human rights law, and she currently teaches in the areas of Land Law and Family Law.

Routledge Research in Human Rights Law

Civilian Drones, Visual Privacy and EU Human Rights Law
Girish Agarwal

International Human Rights Law and Destitution
An Economic, Social and Cultural Rights Perspective
Luke D. Graham

The European Convention of Human Rights Regime
Reform of Immigration and Minority Policies from Afar
Dia Anagnostou

Decisional Privacy and the Rights of the Child
Georgina Dimopoulos

The Rohingya Crisis
Humanitarian and Legal Approaches
Edited by Manzoor Hasan, Syed Mansoob Murshed and Priya Pillai

Sports Investigations Law and the ECHR
Collection, Use and Exchange of Intelligence
Björn Hessert

The Right of the Child to Play
From Conception to Implementation
Naomi Lott

Social Media, Fundamental Rights and Courts
A European Perspective
Edited by Federica Casarosa and Evangelia Psychogiopoulou

Housing, Land and Property Rights
Residential Justice, Conflict Zones and Climate Change
Scott Leckie

For more information about this series, please visit: www.routledge.com/Routledge-Research-in-Human-Rights-Law/book-series/HUMRIGHTSLAW

The European Convention on Human Rights and the COVID-19 Pandemic

Ronagh J.A. McQuigg

Routledge
Taylor & Francis Group
LONDON AND NEW YORK

First published 2024
by Routledge
4 Park Square, Milton Park, Abingdon, Oxon OX14 4RN

and by Routledge
605 Third Avenue, New York, NY 10158

Routledge is an imprint of the Taylor & Francis Group, an informa business

British Library Cataloguing-in-Publication Data
A catalogue record for this book is available from the British Library

Library of Congress Cataloging-in-Publication Data
Names: McQuigg, Ronagh J.A., author.
Title: The European Convention on Human Rights and the Covid-19 andemic / Ronagh J.A. McQuigg.
Description: Abingdon, Oxon [UK]; New York, NY: Routledge, 2024. | Series: Routledge research in human rights law | Includes bibliographical references and index.
Identifiers: LCCN 2023047701 (print) | LCCN 2023047702 (ebook) | ISBN 9781032468068 (hardback) | ISBN 9781032468181 (paperback) | ISBN 9781003383437 (ebook)
Subjects: LCSH: European Court of Human Rights. | Convention for the Protection of Human Rights and Fundamental Freedoms (1950 November 5) | Right to health–Europe. | COVID-19 (Disease)–Law and legislation–Europe. | COVID-19 Pandemic, 2020–Europe.
Classification: LCC KJC5138 .M43 2024 (print) | LCC KJC5138 (ebook) | DDC 341.4/8094–dc23/eng/20231012
LC record available at https://lccn.loc.gov/2023047701
LC ebook record available at https://lccn.loc.gov/2023047702

ISBN: 978-1-032-46806-8 (hbk)
ISBN: 978-1-032-46818-1 (pbk)
ISBN: 978-1-003-38343-7 (ebk)

DOI: 10.4324/9781003383437

Typeset in Times New Roman
by Deanta Global Publishing Services, Chennai, India

Contents

1 Introduction

The COVID-19 pandemic constitutes a crisis which is unprecedented in living memory. At the dawn of 2020, it would have been unimaginable that in just a few short months half of the global population would be in lockdown whilst the world waged war on a deadly new virus.[1] Around four years later, the pandemic is not yet over, but the availability of vaccines has meant that it is being contained.[2] At this stage, thoughts turn to assessing states' responses to the COVID-19 crisis,[3] including the question of the extent to which such responses complied with human rights standards. This book aims to contribute to the emerging body of literature on human rights and the COVID-19 pandemic[4] by providing detailed analysis of the applicability of the provisions of the European Convention on Human Rights (ECHR) to issues raised by the pandemic and an in-depth exploration of the case law of the European

1 Euronews, 'Coronavirus: Half of humanity now on lockdown as 90 countries call for confinement', 3 April 2020, https://www.euronews.com/2020/04/02/coronavirus-in-europe-spain-s-death-toll-hits-10-000-after-record-950-new-deaths-in-24-hou.

2 For information on the total number of cases of COVID-19 reported to the World Health Organization and the total number of vaccine doses administered worldwide, see World Health Organization, 'WHO coronavirus (COVID-19) dashboard', https://covid19.who.int/.

3 For example, the UK COVID-19 Inquiry was set up to 'examine the UK's response to and impact of the COVID-19 pandemic, and learn lessons for the future'. See further https://covid19.public-inquiry.uk/.

4 For example, Kjaerum, M., Davis, M.F. and Lyons, A. (eds), *COVID-19 and Human Rights*, 2021, Routledge, Abingdon; Stanford, B., Foster, S. and Espaliu Berdud, C. (eds), *Global Pandemic, Security and Human Rights*, 2021, Routledge, Abingdon; Chiozza, G. and King, J., 'The state of human rights in a (post) COVID-19 world' (2022) 21 *Journal of Human Rights* 246; Murdie, A., 'Hindsight is 2020: Lessons from the COVID-19 pandemic for future human rights research' (2022) 21 *Journal of Human Rights* 354; Forman, L., and Kohler, J.C., 'Global health and human rights in the time of COVID-19: Response, restrictions, and legitimacy' (2020) 19 *Journal of Human Rights* 547; Wong, W.H. and Wong, E.A., 'What COVID-19 revealed about health, human rights and the WHO' (2020) 19 *Journal of Human Rights* 568; and Shukun, Z., 'International cooperation and human rights protection in the fight against the COVID-19 pandemic' (2021) 20 *Journal of Human Rights* 545.

DOI: 10.4324/9781003383437-1

Court of Human Rights (ECtHR) in this area.[5] The ECHR is one of the few international or regional human rights instruments with a judicial enforcement mechanism, and, indeed, the ECtHR has been described as 'the crown jewel of the world's most advanced international system for protecting civil and political liberties'.[6] As Fraser comments, the ECtHR is 'a unique body that has played a pivotal role in strengthening the protection of human rights across Europe'.[7] Likewise, Bradley remarks that, 'this body has been the foremost regional mechanism in the world for enabling disputed questions of fundamental rights to be decided in a judicial forum'.[8] The approach of the ECtHR to issues raised by the pandemic is, therefore, of great importance and merits detailed exploration.

Also, it is very likely that further pandemics will occur in the future. Scientists have found that the probability of a pandemic with a similar impact to COVID-19 is around 2% in any given year and that the probability of experiencing a pandemic similar to COVID-19 in one's lifetime is, therefore, approximately 38%.[9] Indeed, thoughts have turned to considering how states could be better prepared for the next pandemic. For example, one of the aims of the COVID-19 Inquiry, which has been set up in the UK, is to identify the lessons to be learned from the COVID-19 pandemic in order to inform preparations for future pandemics across the UK,[10] and in September 2022, the World Health Organization produced a report which imagined the future of pandemics and epidemics.[11] It is, therefore, likely that questions similar to those which have arisen concerning the applicability of human rights law generally, and the ECHR more specifically, to issues surrounding the COVID-19 pandemic will arise again in the future – a factor which further emphasises the

5 Some initial analysis can be found in McQuigg, R., 'Responding to a crisis: The European Court of Human Rights and the COVID-19 pandemic' (2022) *European Human Rights Law Review* 283.

6 Helfer, L.R., 'Redesigning the European Court of Human Rights: Embeddedness as a deep structural principle of the European human rights regime' (2008) 19 *European Journal of International Law* 125 at 125.

7 Fraser, J., 'Conclusion: The European Convention on Human Rights as a common European endeavour' in Flogaitis, S., Zwart, T. and Fraser, J. (eds.), *The European Court of Human Rights and its Discontents – Turning Criticism into Strength*, 2013, Edward Elgar Publishing, Cheltenham, 192 at 192.

8 Bradley, A., 'Introduction: The need for both international and national protection of human rights – the European challenge' in Flogaitis, S., Zwart, T. and Fraser, J. (eds.), *The European Court of Human Rights and its Discontents – Turning Criticism into Strength*, 2013, Edward Elgar Publishing, Cheltenham, 1 at 2.

9 Marani, M., Katul, G.G., Pan, W.K and Parolari, A.J., 'Intensity and frequency of extreme novel epidemics', 23 August 2021, *Proceedings of the National Academy of Sciences*, https://www.pnas.org/doi/10.1073/pnas.2105482118.

10 UK COVID-19 Inquiry, https://covid19.public-inquiry.uk/terms-of-reference/.

11 World Health Organization, 'Imagining the future of pandemics and epidemics: A 2022 perspective', 4 September 2022, https://www.who.int/publications/i/item/9789240052093.

necessity for critical analysis to be carried out regarding the applicability of the ECHR to such issues.

The COVID-19 Pandemic and State Responses

Following the identification of the first cases of COVID-19 in December 2019, the virus spread around the globe at an alarming rate. On 30 January 2020, the World Health Organization declared a public health emergency of international concern and proceeded to declare a pandemic on 11 March 2020. And so, the war began – a war fought not against a visible enemy with guns and tanks, but a war fought in hospitals, care homes and private residences against an invisible virus. In such a rapidly developing situation, states had to act quickly, with many imposing a range of unprecedented restrictions, including lockdown measures which permitted individuals to leave their homes only in strictly limited circumstances.[12] For example, UK government guidance stated that people should only leave home to shop for basic necessities such as food and medicine; one form of exercise per day; medical need or to provide care or help to a vulnerable person; and travelling to and from work, but only when work could not be done from home. Even when the activity in question fell within one of these four categories, the amount of time spent away from home had to be minimised as far as possible.[13] In the UK, the oft-repeated mantra was, 'Stay at home; protect the National Health Service (NHS); save lives', and this was exactly what the large majority of people did. Things which had previously been taken for granted – visiting family members, attending church services, going to the hairdresser – suddenly became impermissible, and a situation which many had thought would last only a few weeks stretched to months and then to years. New terms such as 'self-isolation', 'social distancing' and 'track and trace' became embedded into the language; and in common parlance 'Coronavirus' became 'COVID-19' and then simply 'COVID'. Lockdown measures eased at various intervals, although to many this made little difference – the virus remained a threat. At the time of writing, the pandemic is not yet over, but vaccines are a powerful weapon in the fight.

Lockdown measures were indisputably an essential response to the pandemic. For example, at the time when restrictions were implemented in the

12 See for example, the Health Protection (Coronavirus, Restrictions) (England) Regulations 2020 (SI 2020/350).

13 BBC News, 'Coronavirus: Strict new curbs on life in UK announced by PM', 24 March 2020, https://www.bbc.co.uk/news/uk-52012432. See Cabinet Office, 'Guidance: Staying at home and away from others (social distancing)', updated 1 May 2020, https://www.gov.uk/government/publications/full-guidance-on-staying-at-home-and-away-from-others/full-guidance-on-staying-at-home-and-away-from-others.

UK, 335 people in this state had died as a result of contracting COVID-19.[14] This was a deadly new virus about which little was known at the time and for which there was no vaccine. In such circumstances, measures which strictly limited contact were regarded as the only option open to governments to adopt. As was advised by the World Health Organization on 1 April 2020, 'Public health and social measures to slow or stop the spread of COVID-19 must be implemented with the full engagement of all members of society'.[15] The World Health Organization proceeded to state that,

> These measures to reduce transmission of COVID-19 include … social and physical distancing measures including for mass gatherings … While vaccines and specific medications are not yet available for COVID-19, other public health and social measures play an essential role in reducing the number of infections and saving lives. Social and physical distancing measures aim to slow the spread of disease by stopping chains of transmission of COVID-19 and preventing new ones from appearing.[16]

In order to reduce the spread of the virus, the best course of action was to attempt to keep people apart as much as possible. Essentially, in the absence of interaction, a virus cannot spread. From the first cases of the virus that emerged in December 2019 to July 2023, around 770,000,000 confirmed cases of COVID-19 worldwide had been reported to the World Health Organization, with around 7,000,000 deaths as a result of the virus.[17] The number of deaths would undoubtedly have been much higher if restrictive measures had not been implemented by states. As was stated by the World Health Organization on 14 June 2021, 'Public health and social measures (PHSM) have proven critical to limiting transmission of COVID-19 and reducing deaths'.[18]

The ECHR and Responses to the Pandemic

The ECHR was opened for signature in November 1950 and came into force in September 1953. As Thomas and Beasley remark, 'The concept of human rights developed largely from Western political theory of the rights of the

14 BBC News, op. cit.

15 World Health Organization, 'Coronavirus disease 2019 (COVID-19) situation report – 72', 1 April 2020, https://apps.who.int/iris/handle/10665/331685.

16 World Health Organization, 'Coronavirus disease 2019 (COVID-19) situation report – 72', 1 April 2020.

17 World Health Organization, 'WHO Coronavirus (COVID-19) dashboard', https://covid19.who.int/.

18 World Health Organization, 'Considerations for implementing and adjusting public health and social measures in the context of COVID-19 – interim guidance', 14 June 2021, https://apps.who.int/iris/handle/10665/341811.

individual to autonomy and freedom'.[19] The foundation of international relations is the idea of the liberal state. As Romany comments, 'Liberalism constructs a social and political order which seeks to emancipate the individual from the oppression of political structures'.[20] International law, thus, has its basis in the liberal social contract theory, whereby states are regarded as individuals that should have equality, independence and freedom. Inherent to this theory is the idea of negative rights ensuring individual freedom. This concept is, therefore, embedded deeply in the discourse of international law and, subsequently, human rights law.[21] Essentially, the concept of 'negative rights' means that the state cannot interfere with an individual in certain aspects of his or her life.[22]

The idea of negative rights ensuring individual freedoms emerged again during the fight against totalitarianism, which was a vital catalyst in the development of human rights law. The concept of human rights evolved to protect the rights of the individual from encroachment by the state. As Thomas and Beasley remark, 'States are bound by international law to respect the individual rights of each and every person and are thus accountable for abuses of those rights'.[23] However, the norms that emerged with these rights were generally formulated in a very negative manner, whereby the state was required only to refrain from violating the rights in question. There were no obligations on the state to take positive steps to ensure that the rights of the individual were not breached. As Romany comments, the ultimate concern was the separation and protection of the individual from the state.[24] The objective of the framers of the earlier human rights instruments was to ensure that there was a space wherein the individual would be 'left alone' by the state. Their aim was not to obtain positive entitlements from the state.

For example, the ECHR 'arose out of the determination of the signatory States to consign to history the atrocities of the Second World War',[25] and most of its provisions are framed in a negative way with the emphasis being placed on the state's duty of non-interference. Indeed, the ECHR provides one of the clearest examples of the negative formulation of rights that is found in many

19 Thomas, D.Q. and Beasley, M.E., 'Symposium on reconceptualizing violence against women by intimate partners' (1995) 58 *Albany Law Review* 1119 at 1121.

20 Romany, C., 'Women as aliens: A feminist critique of the public/private distinction in international human rights law' (1993) 6 *Harvard Human Rights Journal* 87 at 90.

21 Romany, op. cit., at 89–98.

22 For historical arguments on rights, see Harvey, C., 'Talking about human rights' (2004) *European Human Rights Law Review* 500.

23 Thomas and Beasley, op. cit., at 121.

24 Romany, C., 'State responsibility goes private: A feminist critique of the public/private distinction in international human rights law', in Cook, R.J. (ed.), *Human Rights of Women – National and International Perspectives*, 1994, University of Pennsylvania Press, Philadelphia, 85 at 89.

25 Council of Europe, 'The European Convention on Human Rights – a living instrument', September 2022, https://echr.coe.int/Documents/Convention_Instrument_ENG.pdf, at 9.

human rights instruments. Historically, this negative formulation of rights has caused major difficulties for the effectiveness of international human rights law, as it served to greatly limit the types of situations in which human rights law could be used. Nevertheless, a concept of state responsibility has now been developed, under which positive obligations can be placed directly on the state to ensure that human rights standards are upheld in situations involving only private individuals. This strategy has been utilised to great effect by the ECtHR, which essentially derived this principle from three sources. First, under Article 1 of the ECHR, states parties have a duty to secure the rights to everyone within their jurisdictions. This appears to indicate that states are obliged to take positive steps to ensure that private individuals are able to enjoy their rights freely. Second, it is assumed that rights should be effective, as opposed to being simply theoretical.[26] As Mowbray remarks, 'Passive non-interference by governmental authorities with persons' Convention rights is not sufficient to ensure that many of those rights are fully and effectively respected'.[27] Third, under Article 13 of the Convention, states parties must provide effective remedies for breaches of rights.[28] Again, this provision serves to impose positive obligations on states. The positive duties which may be placed on states parties are wide ranging. Indeed, Starmer explains that the ECtHR has recognised five main categories of obligations which can be imposed: a duty to establish a legal framework providing effective rights protection, an obligation to prevent breaches of rights, a duty to provide information relevant to the rights violation, an obligation to respond to breaches and a duty to provide resources to individuals to prevent violations of their rights.[29]

The ECtHR has repeatedly asserted that the ECHR is a 'living instrument which ... must be interpreted in the light of present-day conditions'.[30] As is commented in a Council of Europe publication,

> What gives the Convention its strength and makes it extremely modern is the way the Court interprets it: dynamically, in the light of present-day conditions. By its case-law the Court has extended the rights set out in the Convention, such that its provisions apply today to situations that were totally unforeseeable and unimaginable at the time it was first adopted.[31]

26 Starmer, K., *European Human Rights Law, the Human Rights Act 1998 and the European Convention on Human Rights*, 1999, LAG, London, at 194.

27 Mowbray, A.R., *The Development of Positive Obligations under the European Convention on Human Rights by the European Court of Human Rights*, 2004, Hart Publishing, Oxford, at 221.

28 Starmer, op. cit., at 194.

29 Starmer, op. cit., at 196.

30 This principle was first stated by the ECtHR in *Tyrer v United Kingdom* (App. No. 5856/72), judgment of 25 April 1978, at para. 31.

31 Council of Europe, op. cit., at 7.

The COVID-19 pandemic is perhaps a paradigm example of a situation which was 'totally unforeseeable and unimaginable' at the time when the ECHR was first adopted. Indeed, even if a global pandemic had somehow been foreseen, it would have been unimaginable to the drafters of the ECHR that the provisions of this instrument could be used to place duties on the state to adopt measures to protect the lives of individuals from a virus, as is discussed in Chapter 2 of this book. This would simply not have come within the concept of rights which prevailed at the time and which involved only the negative duty of non-interference. Interestingly, however, the drafters of the ECHR may have had less difficulty with seeing the relevance of the instrument's provisions to the measures adopted by states in response to the pandemic, as considered in Chapters 3 and 4 of this book. The limitations of rights inherent to many such measures were directly imposed by states, thereby engaging the duty of non-interference which provided the basis for the formulation of human rights instruments such as the ECHR.

It has always been accepted that the application of human rights standards frequently involves a balancing exercise, and nowhere is this more apparent than with the application of ECHR provisions in the context of the COVID-19 pandemic. On the one hand, states were obliged to adopt measures to comply with their positive duties to protect the right to life under Article 2 and the right to be free from torture or inhuman or degrading treatment as found in Article 3, particularly as regards those who were clinically vulnerable to the virus. According to the World Health Organization, 'COVID-19 is often more severe in people who are older than 60 years or who have health conditions like lung or heart disease, diabetes or conditions that affect their immune system'.[32] As was stated in a toolkit for states parties on 'Respecting democracy, rule of law and human rights in the framework of the COVID-19 sanitary crisis', which was issued by the Council of Europe in April 2020,

> responsibility under Articles 2 and 3 of the Convention may be invoked in respect of severely ill patients, people with disabilities or elderly persons … Their exposure to the disease and the extreme level of suffering may be found incompatible with the state's positive obligations to protect life and prevent ill-treatment.[33]

Conversely, however, the measures taken to limit the spread of COVID-19 themselves raise questions regarding human rights. Such measures had an enormous impact on the lives of individuals and caused substantial amounts

32 World Health Organization, 'COVID-19: vulnerable and high risk groups', https://www.who.int/westernpacific/emergencies/covid-19/information/high-risk-groups.

33 Council of Europe, 'Respecting democracy, rule of law and human rights in the framework of the COVID-19 sanitary crisis: A toolkit for member states', 7 April 2020, SG/Inf(2020)11, 5.

of suffering. For example, the mental health of many people was greatly affected,[34] many lost their employment or their businesses,[35] and the lockdown measures increased the suffering of many victims of domestic abuse.[36] In addition, liberties which had previously been taken for granted, such as congregating for public worship, meeting with family and friends and assembling for peaceful protest, were severely limited. The measures which were adopted by states in response to the COVID-19 pandemic engage provisions of the ECHR such as the right to liberty under Article 5; the right to a fair trial under Article 6; the right to respect for private and family life under Article 8; the right to freedom of thought, conscience and religion under Article 9; the right to freedom of expression under Article 10; the right to freedom of assembly and association under Article 11; the right to protection of property under Article 1 of Protocol No. 1; the right to education under Article 2 of Protocol No. 1; and the right to freedom of movement under Article 2 of Protocol No. 4. As was stated in the toolkit for states parties to the ECHR,

> The major social, political and legal challenge facing our member states will be their ability to respond to this crisis effectively, whilst ensuring that the measures they take do not undermine our genuine long-term interest in safeguarding Europe's founding values of democracy, rule of law and human rights.[37]

This book encompasses in-depth discussion of the emerging jurisprudence of the ECtHR relating to issues arising from the pandemic. To date, a substantial number of complaints concerning such issues have been made to the ECtHR. The book analyses such cases which have been examined on their merits as well as the admissibility decisions which have been issued by the Court in this area. In addition, there are a number of relevant pending applications, and discussion of these will also be included. As is apparent from the applications

34 Mental Health Foundation, 'Mental health in the COVID-19 pandemic: Recommendations for prevention', https://www.mentalhealth.org.uk/coronavirus/pandemic-recommendations-prevention.

35 International Labour Organization, 'COVID-19 and the world of work', https://www.ilo.org/global/topics/coronavirus/lang--en/index.htm.

36 World Health Organization, 'COVID-19 and violence against women. What the health sector/system can do', 7 April 2020, https://apps.who.int/iris/bitstream/handle/10665/331699/WHO-SRH-20.04-eng.pdf?ua=1. See also McQuigg, R., 'Domestic abuse: The "shadow pandemic"' (2022) 73 *Northern Ireland Legal Quarterly* 341; and McQuigg, R., 'The COVID-19 pandemic, domestic abuse and human rights' in Deflem, M. (ed.), *Crime and Social Control in Pandemic Times*. (Sociology of Crime, Law, and Deviance, Volume 28), 2023, Emerald Publishing, Bingley, 7.

37 Council of Europe, op. cit., at 2. For discussion of broader issues surrounding human rights in the context of the pandemic, see M. Kjaerum. M.F. Davis and A. Lyons (eds.), *COVID-19 and Human Rights*, 2021, Routledge, Abingdon.

which have been made to date to the ECtHR, human rights claims in the context of the pandemic fall into two broad categories: those based on arguments that states did not put in place sufficient measures to protect individuals from the virus and those entailing arguments that the measures put in place themselves involved breaches of rights. The essential question with which the ECtHR must grapple is how to adjudicate on the correct balance which should have been struck. This book argues that the ECtHR should be cautious of finding breaches of the ECHR in cases involving public restrictions which were applied for the purpose of protecting life and health in response to a global pandemic. If the concept of a human rights violation is defined too broadly, this dilutes the seriousness of such a breach. In particular, it is argued that to preserve the legitimacy of human rights law, the Court must be cautious of applying an overly narrow margin of appreciation in such cases.[38]

From the outset, however, it must be remembered that to engage in any analysis of the applicability of human rights provisions to the issues raised by the COVID-19 pandemic requires a certain degree of self-awareness. Such issues do not relate to abstract questions of human rights law. Rather, they relate to the lived experiences of currently almost every human being on the planet. Every person had their own individualised experience of the pandemic, and the experiences of no two individuals were precisely the same. Some people lost loved ones. Others became extremely ill. Still others contracted the virus and experienced only moderate or mild symptoms or even no symptoms at all, and there are also people who have never contracted COVID-19. For those who were clinically or extremely vulnerable to the virus, and those who lived in their households, by far the main priority was avoiding contracting COVID-19. Although generalisations cannot, of course, be made, it is, nevertheless, likely that such individuals tended to have strong levels of support for the restrictions put in place by states to limit the spread of the virus, demonstrated high levels

38 Discussion surrounding legitimacy and the ECtHR can be found in Dzehtsiarou, K., *European Consensus and the Legitimacy of the European Court of Human Rights*, 2015, Cambridge University Press, Cambridge; and de Londras, F. and Dzehtsiarou, K., *Great Debates on the European Convention on Human Rights*, 2018, Bloomsbury, London. For discussion of the use of the margin of appreciation in the case law of the ECtHR, see Molbæk-Steensig, H., 'Subsidarity does not win cases: A mixed methods study of the relationship between margin of appreciation language and deference at the European Court of Human Rights' (2023) 36 *Leiden Journal of International Law* 83; Tripkovic, B., 'A new philosophy for the margin of appreciation and European consensus' (2022) *Oxford Journal of Legal Studies* 207; Trykhlib, K.O., 'The scope of the margin of appreciation in the jurisprudence of the European Court of Human Rights' (2021) 154 *Problems of Legality* 65; Brems, E., 'Positive subsidiarity and its implications for the margin of appreciation doctrine' (2019) 37 *Netherlands Quarterly of Human Rights* 210; Vogiatzis, N., 'The relationship between European consensus, the margin of appreciation and the legitimacy of the Strasbourg Court' (2019) 25 *European Public Law* 445; Greer, S., *The Margin of Appreciation: Interpretation and Discretion under the European Convention on Human Rights*, 2000, Council of Europe, Strasbourg; and Yourow, H.C., *The Margin of Appreciation Doctrine in the Dynamics of European Human Rights Jurisprudence*, 1996, Kluwer Law International, The Hague.

of compliance with such restrictions and may frequently have been of the view that such restrictions were loosened or lifted at too early a stage. Indeed, many such individuals did not only adhere to such restrictions but also demonstrated a far greater degree of care than was actually required by law. In terms of the applicability of the ECHR to issues raised by the pandemic, it is likely that such people would view the need to protect life and health as being the paramount consideration and that human-rights-based challenges to the restrictive measures put in place by states should be seen as unfounded.

Conversely, there were other individuals who had a very different experience of the COVID-19 pandemic. Those not in the clinically vulnerable groups and who had no members of their households in such groups may not have been so anxious to avoid contracting the virus. For such people, the main impact on their lives may have been caused not by the threat of the virus itself but, rather, by the restrictions put in place by governments to prevent and limit the spread of the virus. Again, the precise extent of this impact varied depending on individual circumstances. For example, in the sphere of employment, the pandemic gave some the opportunity to work from home, which many enjoyed. On the other hand, for others, the pandemic had a devastating impact financially in terms of job loss. For school pupils who had to move to online learning, some enjoyed the opportunity to learn remotely from home, whilst others keenly missed their peers and the levels of support normally provided by teachers during in-person lessons. Likewise, rules which prevented meeting with people from other households had less of an impact on those who lived with those closest to them than they did on those who had very close family members with whom they did not share a household. Again, sweeping generalisations cannot and should not be made; however, it is perhaps more likely that individuals whose lives were impacted greatly in a very negative way by the restrictions put in place may be more likely to support arguments that such measures may violate provisions of human rights law. For those who have lived through the pandemic, whatever one's experience, it is likely that absolute objectivity in such matters may be somewhat difficult to achieve.

Derogations from the ECHR in the Pandemic Context

Article 15(1) of the ECHR allows states, 'in time of war or other public emergency threatening the life of the nation' to adopt measures derogating from their duties under the Convention 'to the extent strictly required by the exigencies of the situation', provided that such measures are not inconsistent with the state's other duties under international law.[39] Under Article 15(2), deroga-

39 For discussion generally of the use of derogations from the ECHR, see Wallace, S., 'Derogations from the European Convention on Human Rights: The case for reform' (2020) 20 *Human Rights Law Review* 769.

tions are not permitted from Article 2 (except as regards deaths resulting from lawful acts of war), Article 3, the prohibition of slavery under Article 4(1), or Article 7, which provides that no one shall be held guilty of any criminal offence on account of any act or omission which did not constitute a criminal offence at the time when it was committed. Notably, in March/April 2020, ten states chose to enter derogations in respect of the measures which they were adopting due to the pandemic.[40] Interestingly, and for no reason that is immediately apparent, all of the states which entered derogations, with the exception of San Marino, are eastern European states. All of these derogations have now been withdrawn.

However, the large majority of the states parties to the ECHR chose not to enter derogations in relation to the measures which they took in response to COVID-19. Under the ECHR, a number of the rights contained therein can be limited in certain circumstances. For example, with regard to the right to respect for private and family life under Article 8(1), Article 8(2) states that, 'There shall be no interference by a public authority with the exercise of this right except such as is in accordance with the law and is necessary in a democratic society' for a range of reasons, including 'the protection of health' and 'the protection of the rights and freedoms of others'. Likewise, the rights contained in Articles 9, 10 and 11 can all be restricted for reasons including protecting health and protecting the rights and freedoms of others. It seems that the states which did not enter derogations chose to rely on such clauses.[41]

Nevertheless, it is by no means clear where the line is drawn between a permissible restriction under such a limitation clause and a matter which would go beyond this and require a derogation to be entered. As noted above, Article 15(1) allows states, in time of public emergency threatening the life of the nation, to adopt measures derogating from their obligations under the ECHR 'to the extent strictly required by the exigencies of the situation'. As Hickman comments, the 'strictly required' standard 'has a rather puzzling place in the

40 Albania, Armenia, Estonia, Georgia, Latvia, North Macedonia, the Republic of Moldova, Romania, San Marino and Serbia. The notifications under Article 15 in the context of the COVID-19 pandemic are available at https://www.coe.int/en/web/conventions/derogations-covid-19.

41 For discussion from early in the pandemic of whether derogations from the ECHR were necessary, see Dzehtsiarou, K., 'Article 15 Derogations: Are they really necessary during the COVID-19 Pandemic?'(2020) *European Human Rights Law Review* 359; Greene, A., 'On the Value of Derogations from the European Convention on Human Rights in response to the COVID-19 Pandemic: a Rejoinder' (2020) *European Human Rights Law Review* 526; and Hickman, T., 'The Coronavirus Pandemic and Derogation from the European Convention on Human Rights' (2020) *European Human Rights Law Review* 593. For discussion of derogations from the International Covenant on Civil and Political Rights in the context of the pandemic, see Qiu, D., 'Human Rights Protection under the ICCPR: When Can and Should States Derogate? A Critical Analysis in the Context of New Zealand's COVID-19 Response' (2022) *International Journal of Human Rights*, DOI: 10.1080/13642987.2022.2066080.

scheme of the ECHR as a whole'.[42] Essentially, 'it introduces a requirement that seems to duplicate the proportionality standard'.[43] As Hickman states,

> By not carving out a clear or distinct space between the operation of art. 15 and limitation clauses contained in arts 8–11, as well as by its attachment to a generic concept of proportionality, the Court's approach is not always easy to make sense of.[44]

In retrospect, however, it appears that when assessing measures adopted by states in response to the pandemic, the ECtHR may afford a wider margin of appreciation to states which entered derogations than to those which did not. As discussed in Chapter 3 of this book, there is some support for this conclusion in the judgment of the ECtHR in *Communauté Genevoise D'Action Syndicale (CGAS) v Switzerland.*[45] In this case, in which the applicant argued that a prohibition of public gatherings violated its right to freedom of assembly under Article 11, the Court referred to the fact that Switzerland had not entered a derogation and, therefore, was obliged to comply fully with Article 11, within the margin of appreciation afforded to it.

In any event, the essential point remains that issues surrounding measures adopted by states parties in response to the pandemic and their compliance to the ECHR do not hinge on the question of whether they restricted the rights therein – they undoubtedly did – but, rather, they relate to the question of whether these restrictions were legitimate. In the toolkit for states parties to the ECHR, which was issued in April 2020, it was noted that, 'It is for each state to assess whether the measures it adopts warrant … a derogation, depending on the nature and extent of restrictions applied to the rights and freedoms protected by the Convention'.[46]

Interim Measures

Under Rule 39 of the Rules of Court of the ECtHR, the Court may indicate interim measures to any state party to the ECHR.[47] These are urgent meas-

42 Hickman, op. cit., at 597.
43 Hickman, op. cit., at 597.
44 Hickman, op. cit., at 600.
45 App. No. 21881/20, judgment of 15 March 2022.
46 Council of Europe, op. cit., at 2.
47 Rule 39(1) states that, 'The Chamber or, where appropriate, the President of the Section or a duty judge appointed pursuant to paragraph 4 of this Rule may, at the request of a party or of any other person concerned, or of their own motion, indicate to the parties any interim measure which they consider should be adopted in the interests of the parties or of the proper conduct of the proceedings'. The Rules of Court of the ECtHR are available at https://www.echr.coe.int/documents/rules_court_eng.pdf.

ures which apply only when there is an imminent risk of irreparable harm. Such measures are decided in connection with proceedings before the ECtHR and do not prejudge any subsequent decisions on the admissibility or merits of the case in question. Requests for interim measures are most commonly made in the context of applicants seeking the suspension of an expulsion or extradition.[48] However, between March 2020 and July 2022, the ECtHR processed approximately 370 requests for interim measures which related to the COVID-19 pandemic. A detailed study of these requests is beyond the scope of this book; however, it is notable that the majority of such requests were brought by individuals who were detained in prison or in detention centres for asylum seekers and migrants and who wished for interim measures to be applied entailing that they be removed from their place of detention or that steps be taken to protect them from contracting the COVID-19 virus. Many of these requests for interim measures were rejected, although, in some cases, the ECtHR adjourned its decision and requested information from the state in question.[49]

The ECtHR also received requests for interim measures from medical professionals, employees working in medical facilities and firefighters, who challenged compulsory vaccination schemes, and from individuals who challenged the use of COVID-19 certificates which stipulated that only those in possession of such certificates would be allowed to attend public places and, in some cases, to use public transport. However, all such requests were rejected as being outside the scope of application of Rule 39. There were also a small number of requests for general measures, such as the enforcement of a total lockdown in particular cities, bur these requests were also rejected.[50]

Chapter Outline

As noted above, ECHR claims in the context of the pandemic fall into two broad categories: those based on arguments that states did not put in place sufficient measures to protect individuals from the virus and those entailing arguments that the measures put in place themselves involved breaches of rights. The book's structure reflects this, in that Chapter 2 addresses the duties of the state to provide protection from COVID-19 under Articles 2 and 3 of the ECHR, whilst Chapters 3 and 4 proceed to address the human rights implications of the measures which were put in place to this end.

At an early stage in the pandemic, the World Health Organization stated that, 'Public health and social measures to slow or stop the spread of

48 Press Unit, European Court of Human Rights, 'Factsheet – interim measures', August 2022, https://www.echr.coe.int/documents/fs_interim_measures_eng.pdf, 1.

49 Press Unit, European Court of Human Rights, op. cit., at 12.

50 Press Unit, European Court of Human Rights, op. cit., at 12–13.

COVID-19 must be implemented with the full engagement of all members of society'.[51] As is discussed in Chapter 2, the implementation of such measures was necessary in order for states to comply with their positive duties to protect the right to life, as found in Article 2 of the ECHR, and the right to be free from torture or inhuman or degrading treatment, as found in Article 3, particularly as regards those who were clinically vulnerable to the virus. In addition, as was stated by the Council of Europe Commissioner for Human Rights in April 2020,

> Convicted prisoners and persons on remand are among those most vulnerable to viral contagion as they are held in a high-risk environment: in general, detention facilities are not adapted to face large-scale epidemics, and the basic protective measures such as social distancing and hygiene rules cannot be observed as easily as outside, exposing prisoners to greater health risks.[52]

Chapter 2 examines decisions of the ECtHR relating to claims that states did not adopt sufficient measures to provide adequate protection against COVID-19, such as *Feilazoo v Malta*,[53] *Fenech v Malta*[54] and *Le Mailloux v France*.[55] In addition, there are currently a number of pending applications relating to such claims.[56]

In contrast to Chapter 2, which focuses on the duties of the state to provide protection from COVID-19, Chapters 3 and 4 turn to the human rights implications of the measures which were put in place to this end. As is discussed in Chapter 3, generally one of the most prominent aspects of the responses of states to the pandemic was to put in place measures prohibiting or restricting public gatherings. Such measures raise issues in relation to the right to freedom of assembly and association under Article 11 of the ECHR as well as the right to freedom of expression under Article 10, in the case of public

51 World Health Organization, 'Coronavirus disease 2019 (COVID-19) situation report – 72', 1 April 2020, https://apps.who.int/iris/handle/10665/331685.

52 Council of Europe Commissioner for Human Rights, 'COVID-19 pandemic: Urgent steps are needed to protect the rights of prisoners in Europe', 6 April 2020, https://www.coe.int/en/web/commissioner/-/covid-19-pandemic-urgent-steps-are-needed-to-protect-the-rights-of-prisoners-in-europe.

53 App. No. 6865/19, judgment of 11 March 2021.

54 App. No. 19090/20, judgment of 1 March 2022.

55 App. No. 18108/20, decision of 5 November 2020.

56 For example, *Maratsis and Others v Greece*, App. No. 39335/20; *Vasilakis and Others v Greece*, App. No. 30379/20; *Vlamis and Others v Greece*, App. Nos. 29655/20, 29689/20, 30240/20, 30418/20 and 30574/20; *Rus v Romania*, App. No. 2621/21; *Riela v Italy*, App. No. 17378/20; *Faia v Italy*, App. No. 17222/20; *Hafeez v the United Kingdom*, App. No. 14198/20; and *Krstic v Serbia*, App. No. 35246/21.

gatherings for the purpose of peaceful protest, and the right to freedom of religion under Article 9, in the case of gatherings for collective worship.

A prohibition of public gatherings in response to the pandemic was the subject of *Communauté Genevoise D'Action Syndicale (CGAS) v Switzerland*,[57] a case in which the ECtHR issued an important judgment on 15 March 2022, and which is considered in detail in this chapter. In this case the applicant, an association with the aim of defending the interests of workers and trade unions, argued that the prohibition in question breached Article 11. The ECtHR held that the interference with the rights protected by Article 11 had not been proportionate to the aims pursued and that there had, thus, been a violation of this provision. The decision was not unanimous, however, and it is argued that the approach of the dissenting judges was, in fact, correct. Essentially the ECtHR should be cautious of finding breaches of the ECHR in cases involving public restrictions which were applied for the purpose of protecting life and health in response to a global pandemic. It has been established by the ECtHR that when there is no consensus among states parties, a wider margin of appreciation should be afforded.[58] There was certainly no consensus among states parties against the type of measure in question in *CGAS* – any consensus was actually in favour of this type of measure given that it appears to have been very much in line with those imposed by many other states in Europe and beyond. Indeed, it is submitted that cases such as *CGAS* constitute paradigm examples of an area in which a wide margin of appreciation should be granted to states. The *CGAS* case has, however, been referred to the Grand Chamber at the request of the Swiss government, and a hearing was held on 12 April 2023. It remains to be seen whether the significant difficulties with the first instance judgment of the ECtHR in this case will be remedied by the judgment of the Grand Chamber.

As is also discussed in Chapter 3, there are currently a number of applications pending before the ECtHR which raise similar issues to those considered in *CGAS*. For example, in *Central Unitaria de Traballadores/as v Spain*,[59] the applicant argues that the right to organise and take part in a peaceful demonstration had been breached during the pandemic, contrary to Articles 10 and 11, and in *Jarocki v Poland*,[60] the applicant complains that a refusal to authorise a demonstration involving 1,000 participants that he wished to hold

57 App. No. 21881/20, judgment of 15 March 2022.

58 As was stated by the Grand Chamber in *Dickson v the United Kingdom*, 'Where … there is no consensus within the member States of the Council of Europe either as to the relative importance of the interest at stake or as to how best to protect it, the margin will be wider'. (App. No. 44362/04, judgment of 4 December 2007, at para. 78).

59 App. No. 49363/20.

60 App. No. 39750/20. See also the pending applications of *Nemytov v Russia*, App. No. 1257/21; *Azar v Russia*, App. No. 3244/21; and *Kostyukhin v Russia*, App. No. 24699/21, all of which relate to a prohibition of public events in Moscow which was introduced as a response to the pandemic.

in August 2020 violated Article 11. However, with its decision in *CGAS*, the ECtHR may already have taken a wrong turn and embarked upon a problematic course from which retreat may be difficult.

Prior to the judgment of the ECtHR in *CGAS*, the compatibility with Article 11 of restrictions on public gatherings in the context of the pandemic had been considered by the domestic courts in the UK. In *R (Dolan) v Secretary of State for Health and Social Care*,[61] the appellants challenged regulations[62] made on 26 March 2020, which they submitted imposed restrictions which were unlawful on various grounds including that they violated Articles 5, 8, 9 and 11 of the ECHR and Articles 1 and 2 of Protocol No. 1, all of which are guaranteed in domestic law under the Human Rights Act 1998. The appellants sought permission to apply for judicial review of the regulations; however, this was refused by Lewis J. in the High Court, who held that there had been no violation of any of the ECHR rights in question. This finding was then upheld by the Court of Appeal. The Article 11 challenge, in this case, related to Regulation 7, which, in its original form, prohibited gatherings in a public place of more than two people (unless the people were members of the same household or the gathering was for specified purposes such as work). The regulation was later amended to the effect that from 1 June 2020, gatherings of more than six people in a public place, or more than two people indoors, were prohibited unless the people were from the same household. Interestingly, in considering the compatibility of these measures with Article 11, the UK courts adopted a position which was diametrically opposed to the approach later taken by the ECtHR in *CGAS.* As in the *CGAS* case, it was accepted in *Dolan* that the measures in question certainly involved a restriction of the right to freedom of assembly and association under Article 11. However, the courts in *Dolan* were strongly of the view that the restriction was a proportionate response to the legitimate aims being pursued. As Lewis J. commented, 'there is no realistic prospect of a court deciding in these, possibly unique, circumstances that the regulation was a disproportionate interference with the rights guaranteed by Article 11 of the Convention'.[63] Somewhat ironically, around two years after the judgment of Lewis J. was issued, a court, namely the ECtHR, did find that restrictions, which were arguably less stringent than those at issue in *Dolan*, indeed constituted a disproportionate interference with the rights guaranteed by Article 11. At one level, it is, perhaps, unsurprising that domestic courts may take a more restrictive approach to the scope of Article 11 than that adopted by the ECtHR, which is, of course, the judicial enforcement mechanism of the ECHR itself. Nevertheless, it seems that the

61 [2020] EWHC 1786 (Admin); [2020] EWCA Civ 1605.
62 The Health Protection (Coronavirus, Restrictions) (England) Regulations 2020 (SI 2020/350).
63 [2020] EWHC 1786 (Admin), at paras. 95–96.

approach of the UK courts in *Dolan* has more to commend it than that of the ECtHR in *CGAS*, as is also discussed in Chapter 3.

The restrictions on public gatherings which many states imposed often involved prohibitions on gatherings for collective worship and questions surrounding the compatibility of such restrictions with Article 9 of the ECHR have been raised before the ECtHR in the pending applications of *Association of Orthodox Ecclesiastical Obedience v Greece*,[64] *Megard v France*[65] and *Figel' v Slovakia*.[66] Although the ECtHR has not yet made a ruling on the compatibility with Article 9 of such prohibitions on gatherings for collective worship, it is, nevertheless, noteworthy, as is also explored in Chapter 3, that questions surrounding the extent to which the forced closure of places of worship in Scotland due to the pandemic was compatible with Article 9 have been considered by the Court of Session of Scotland in the case of *Philip and Others for Judicial Review of the closure of places of worship in Scotland*.[67]

The measures adopted by states in response to the COVID-19 pandemic were not, of course, limited to restrictions on public gatherings; rather, they impacted upon the lives of individuals in a wide range of other ways which also engaged various provisions of the ECHR and in relation to which issues have been raised before the ECtHR, as is discussed in Chapter 4. For example, during April 2020, almost half of the world's population were in lockdown,[68] which meant that people could only leave their homes for a very limited range of reasons. Arguments based on Article 5 of the ECHR and Article 2 of Protocol No. 4 relating to such measures have been raised before the ECtHR in cases such as *Terhes v Romania*[69] and *Magdic v Croatia*.[70]

Another common feature of the measures adopted by states because of the pandemic involved schools being required to teach pupils, partly or wholly, through online methods as opposed to in-person classes. In the pending application of *M.C.K. and M.H.K.-B. and Others v Germany*,[71] the applicants are pupils who attended schools which had been subject to such requirements and who argue that these restrictions violated their rights under Article 8 of the ECHR and Article 2 of Protocol No. 1. Although the ECtHR has not yet made a ruling in this case, similar issues to those being raised in *M.C.K. and M.H.K.-B. and Others* were considered by the Court of Appeal of England and Wales in *Dolan*,[72] as is examined in Chapter 4.

64 App. No. 52104/20.
65 App. No. 32647/22.
66 App. No. 12131/21.
67 [2021] CSOH 32, paras. 95–127.
68 Euronews, op. cit.
69 App. No. 49933/20, decision of 20 May 2021.
70 App. No. 17578/20, decision of 5 July 2022.
71 App. No. 26657/22.
72 [2020] EWCA Civ 1605.

As lockdown measures eased, many states imposed a 'health pass' system as an interim stage between lockdown and full easing of the COVID-19 restrictions. Under such systems, individuals were typically required to show proof of vaccination against COVID-19, proof of having recently recovered from COVID-19 or evidence of having tested negative for the virus in order to enter certain premises such as restaurants and other hospitality venues. The compatibility of such measures with the provisions of the ECHR was the subject of the admissibility decision in *Zambrano v France*,[73] as is also considered in Chapter 4. Additionally, during the pandemic, many states imposed requirements to wear face coverings when in indoor public settings, such as shops, as a way of limiting the spread of the virus. Questions surrounding the compatibility of requirements to wear masks have been raised before the ECtHR in *Piperea v Romania*[74] and *Makovetskyy v Ukraine*.[75]

Another type of measure which was adopted in a number of states in response to the pandemic was a requirement for those employed in certain sectors to be vaccinated against COVID-19. For example, in *Thevenon v France*,[76] the applicant argued that his rights under Articles 8 and 14 of the ECHR and Article 1 of Protocol No. 1 had been breached by his suspension from the fire service without pay due to his refusal to be vaccinated against COVID-19.[77] Other measures adopted because of the pandemic also impacted upon individuals in relation to their employment and professional activity. For example, in *Toromag, s.r.o and Others v Slovakia*,[78] the applicants were owners of fitness centres which were closed because of measures taken to prevent the spread of COVID-19. They argued that their rights under Article 1 of Protocol No. 1 were violated due to the alleged pecuniary damage incurred and the loss of future income and clientele. The compatibility with the ECHR of restrictions on professional activities imposed in the context of the pandemic was also considered by the domestic courts in the UK in *Dolan*.

In addition, whilst states had particular duties under Articles 2 and 3 to adopt protective measures against COVID-19 in respect of prisoners and detainees, as is discussed in Chapter 2, it is also the case that measures adopted to prevent the spread of the virus raised particular human rights issues for such persons. In this context, the case of *Fenech v Malta*[79] abundantly

73 App. No. 41994/21, decision of 7 October 2021.

74 App. No. 24183/21, decision of 5 July 2022.

75 App. No. 50824/21, decision of 19 May 2022. See also the pending applications of *Arus v Romania* App. No. 39647/21; *Danijel Grgicin v Croatia*, App. No. 6749/22; and *Liam Grgicin v Croatia*, App. No. 7154/22, all of which concern circumstances relating to requirements to wear masks in the context of the pandemic.

76 App. No. 46061/21.

77 See also the pending application of *Pasquinelli and Others v San Marino*, App. No. 24622/22 in which similar issues are raised.

78 App. Nos. 41217/20, 41253/20, 41263/20, 41271/20 and 49716/20.

79 App. No. 19090/20, judgment of 1 March 2022.

illustrates the two broad categories into which ECHR claims fall – those based on arguments that states did not put in place sufficient measures to protect individuals from the virus and those entailing arguments that the measures put in place themselves involved breaches of rights – in that both types of claim were made in this instance. The applicant, who had been remanded in custody, argued that there had been violations of Articles 2 and 3 on the grounds that sufficient measures had not been taken to protect him from contracting COVID-19. However, as is discussed in Chapter 4, he also alleged that a number of the measures which had been taken were themselves in breach of Article 3, in that, for a certain period of time, he had had no access to the gym, to his family or to other activities. In the case of *Constantin-Lucian Spînu v Romania*,[80] the applicant had been in prison since June 2019. Until February 2020, he had been permitted to leave the prison to attend Adventist Church services. In July 2020, he applied to the prison authorities for permission to attend a service every Saturday; however, his request was denied because of restrictive measures put in place due to the pandemic. The applicant complained that this constituted a violation of his right to freedom of religion under Article 9 of the ECHR; however, no violation of this provision was found by the ECtHR, as is also considered in Chapter 4. There are, in addition, currently a number of pending applications in which arguments are being made that measures adopted in response to the pandemic impacted upon criminal proceedings in ways which violated the ECHR.[81]

As is further discussed in Chapter 4, issues have been raised before the ECtHR relating to the impact on asylum seekers of measures adopted by states due to the COVID-19 pandemic. In the admissibility decision of *Bah v the Netherlands*,[82] a detainee argued that his Article 5 right had been breached, as it had been impossible for him to attend his immigration detention appeal in person because of measures adopted in response to the pandemic or to be heard by tele- or videoconferencing due to infrastructure problems at the beginning of the pandemic. *E.B. v Serbia*[83] and *A.A. v Serbia*[84] are pending applications which concern a temporary restriction on freedom of movement, between 1 March and 14 May 2020, of refugees, asylum seekers and migrants accommodated in asylum and reception centres in Serbia. The applicants, who are asylum seekers, argue that the de facto 24-hour lockdown in the asylum centre in which they had been staying was tantamount to house arrest and, therefore, constituted an unlawful, arbitrary, unnecessary and collective deprivation of liberty in violation of Article 5. The applicants argue that the

80 App. No.29443/20, judgment of 11 October 2022.

81 *Khokhlov v Cyprus*, App. No. 53114/20; *Ait Oufella v France*, App. No. 51860/20; and *Dumea v Romania*, App. No. 6457/21.

82 App. No. 35751/20, decision of 22 June 2021.

83 App. No. 50086/20.

84 App. No. 50898/20.

contested measures were imposed on the basis of discriminatory criteria, in breach of the Article 14 non-discrimination provision, as they unjustifiably distinguished between refugees, asylum seekers and migrants accommodated in asylum and reception centres and the general population of Serbia and asylum seekers residing in private accommodation.

Chapter 5 summarises the key points and conclusions from the preceding analysis. The discussion looks ahead to how the ECtHR may address questions which have not yet been resolved relating to issues arising from the pandemic and provides observations on how such matters should be approached. If the concept of a human rights violation is defined too broadly, this dilutes the seriousness of such a breach. In particular, it is argued that to preserve the legitimacy of human rights law, the Court must be cautious of applying an overly narrow margin of appreciation in such cases. The discourse of human rights is currently coming under sustained questioning. As De Búrca comments, 'Prominent scholars and public intellectuals have variously dismissed the language, ideals, practices, and achievements of human rights law and advocacy as flawed, inadequate, hegemonic, confining, overreaching, apolitical, peripheral, or pointless'.[85] In order to avoid criticism relating to 'the overreach of human rights law',[86] it is argued that the ECtHR should be cautious of finding breaches of the ECHR in cases involving public restrictions which were applied for the purpose of protecting life and health in response to a global pandemic.

85 De Búrca, G., *Reframing Human Rights in a Turbulent Era*, 2021, Oxford University Press, Oxford, at 2.

86 De Búrca, op. cit., at 4. See further Hannum, H., *Rescuing Human Rights: A Radically Moderate Approach*, 2019, Cambridge University Press, Cambridge.

2 The ECHR and Duties to Provide Protection from COVID-19

As was discussed in Chapter 1, ECHR claims in the context of the pandemic fall into two broad categories: those based on arguments that states did not put in place sufficient measures to protect individuals from the virus and those entailing arguments that the measures put in place themselves involved breaches of rights. Chapter 2 addresses the first category of claims and discusses the duties of the state to provide protection from COVID-19. Chapters 3 and 4 proceed to address the human rights implications of the measures which were put in place to this end.

Chapter 2 begins by discussing the obligations on states entailed by Article 2 (the right to life) and Article 3 (the right to be free from torture or inhuman or degrading treatment) of the ECHR to adopt measures to protect individuals from COVID-19. These duties were particularly pertinent in respect of persons who were clinically vulnerable to the virus, such as those who were elderly or who had underlying health conditions. However, there were other categories of individuals who were also at greater risk from COVID-19 due to their circumstances, such as those in detention facilities, and toward whom states, therefore, had particular duties to ensure that their rights under Articles 2 and 3 were not breached in the context of the pandemic.

The chapter then proceeds to examine decisions of the ECtHR relating to claims that states did not adopt sufficient measures to provide adequate protection against COVID-19, such as *Feilazoo v Malta*,[1] *Fenech v Malta*[2] and *Le Mailloux v France*.[3] In addition, there are currently a number of pending applications relating to such claims, such as *Maratsis and Others v Greece*,[4] *Vasilakis and Others v Greece*,[5] *Vlamis and Others v Greece*,[6] *Rus*

1 App. No. 6865/19, judgment of 11 March 2021.
2 App. No. 19090/20, judgment of 1 March 2022.
3 App. No. 18108/20, decision of 5 November 2020.
4 App. No. 39335/20.
5 App. No. 30379/20.
6 App. Nos. 29655/20, 29689/20, 30240/20, 30418/20 and 30574/20.

DOI: 10.4324/9781003383437-2

v Romania,[7] *Riela v Italy,*[8] *Faia v Italy,*[9] *Hafeez v the United Kingdom*[10] and *Krstic v Serbia.*[11]

State Obligations to Provide Protection from COVID-19

Following the identification of the first cases of COVID-19 in December 2019, the virus spread around the globe at an alarming rate. The World Health Organization declared a public health emergency of international concern on 30 January 2020 and then proceeded to declare a pandemic on 11 March 2020. At a media briefing on that date, the Director-General of the World Health Organization stated that,

> There are now more than 118,000 cases [of COVID-19] in 114 countries, and 4,291 people have lost their lives. Thousands more are fighting for their lives in hospitals. In the days and weeks ahead, we expect to see the number of cases, the number of deaths, and the number of affected countries climb even higher. WHO has been assessing this outbreak around the clock and we are deeply concerned … by the alarming levels of spread and severity … We have rung the alarm bell loud and clear.[12]

Essentially, it was abundantly clear that COVID-19 was a deadly virus regarding which the World Health Organization was deeply concerned. Although the majority of those who contract COVID-19 will recover without requiring hospital treatment, 'Complications leading to death may include respiratory failure, acute respiratory distress syndrome (ARDS), sepsis and septic shock, thromboembolism, and/or multiorgan failure, including injury of the heart, liver or kidneys'.[13] In addition, those who have had COVID-19, even if they did not need hospitalisation, may, nevertheless, experience long-term effects, such as respiratory and neurological symptoms and fatigue.[14] As the then Prime Minister of the UK, Boris Johnson, stated on 23 March 2020, 'The coronavirus is the biggest threat this country has faced for decades – and this

7 App. No. 2621/21.
8 App. No. 17378/20.
9 App. No. 17222/20.
10 App. No. 14198/20.
11 App. No. 35246/21.
12 World Health Organization, 'WHO Director-General's opening remarks at the media briefing on COVID-19 – 11 March 2020', https://www.who.int/director-general/speeches/detail/who-director-general-s-opening-remarks-at-the-media-briefing-on-covid-19---11-march-2020.
13 World Health Organization, 'Coronavirus disease (COVID-19)', 13 May 2021, https://www.who.int/emergencies/diseases/novel-coronavirus-2019/question-and-answers-hub/q-a-detail/coronavirus-disease-covid-19.
14 World Health Organization (2021), op. cit.

country is not alone. All over the world we are seeing the devastating impact of this invisible killer'.[15]

Given the immense threat posed by the COVID-19 virus, it was clear that drastic action was needed on the part of states. On 11 March 2020, the Director-General of the World Health Organization expressed deep concern regarding 'the alarming levels of inaction' and pointed out that the World Health Organization had 'called every day for countries to take urgent and aggressive action'.[16] As the then UK Prime Minister stated, 'Without a huge national effort to halt the growth of this virus, there will come a moment when no health service in the world could possibly cope; because there won't be enough ventilators, enough intensive care beds, enough doctors and nurses'.[17] As was asserted by the World Health Organization in April 2020,

> While vaccines and specific medications are not yet available for COVID-19, other public health and social measures play an essential role in reducing the number of infections and saving lives. Social and physical distancing measures aim to slow the spread of disease by stopping chains of transmission of COVID-19 and preventing new ones from appearing.

The World Health Organization proceeded to state that,

> Measures for the general public include introducing flexible work arrangements such as teleworking, distance learning, reducing and avoiding crowding, closure of non-essential facilities and services, shielding and protection for vulnerable groups, local or national movement restrictions and staying-at home measures, and coordinated reorganization of health care and social services networks to protect hospitals … To be effective, public health measures must be implemented with the full engagement of all members of society, including communities and professional groups.[18]

Many states imposed a range of unprecedented restrictions including lock-down measures which permitted individuals to leave their homes only for a strictly limited range of reasons.[19] In April 2020, it was reported that more

15 UK government, 'Prime Minister's statement on coronavirus (COVID-19): 23 March 2020' https://www.gov.uk/government/speeches/pm-address-to-the-nation-on-coronavirus-23-march-2020.
16 World Health Organization (2021), op. cit.
17 UK government, op. cit.
18 World Health Organization, 'Coronavirus disease 2019 (COVID-19) situation report – 72', 1 April 2020, https://apps.who.int/iris/handle/10665/331685.
19 See for example, the Health Protection (Coronavirus, Restrictions) (England) Regulations 2020 (SI 2020/350).

than 3.9 billion people, or half of the global population, were in lockdown.[20] For example, UK government guidance stated that people should only leave home for very limited reasons: shopping for basic necessities such as food and medicine; one form of exercise per day; medical need, or to provide care or help to a vulnerable person; and travelling to and from work, but only when work could not be done from home. Even when the activity in question fell within one of these four categories, the amount of time spent away from home had to be minimised as much as possible.[21]

Indeed, for states parties to the ECHR, the implementation of measures in response to COVID-19 was necessary in order for states to comply with their positive duties to protect the right to life as found in Article 2 of the ECHR and the right to be free from torture or inhuman or degrading treatment as found in Article 3, particularly as regards those who were clinically vulnerable to the virus. Although anyone can, of course, become seriously ill or die as a result of contracting COVID-19, individuals who are aged 60 years and over and those with underlying medical conditions, such as heart and lung problems, obesity or diabetes, are at higher risk of developing serious illness.[22] As was stated in a toolkit for member states on 'Respecting democracy, rule of law and human rights in the framework of the COVID-19 sanitary crisis' which was issued by the Council of Europe in April 2020,

> responsibility under Articles 2 and 3 of the Convention may be invoked in respect of severely ill patients, people with disabilities or elderly persons … Their exposure to the disease and the extreme level of suffering may be found incompatible with the state's positive obligations to protect life and prevent ill-treatment.[23]

In March 2020, the Council of Europe Commissioner for Human Rights stated that,

> The ongoing coronavirus (COVID-19) outbreak is especially dangerous for older persons and has a disproportionately negative impact on their

20 Euronews, 'Coronavirus: Half of humanity now on lockdown as 90 countries call for confinement', 3 April 2020, https://www.euronews.com/2020/04/02/coronavirus-in-europe-spain-s-death-toll-hits-10-000-after-record-950-new-deaths-in-24-hou.

21 BBC News, 'Coronavirus: Strict new curbs on life in UK announced by PM', 24 March 2020, https://www.bbc.co.uk/news/uk-52012432. See Cabinet Office, 'Guidance: Staying at home and away from others (social distancing)', updated 1 May 2020, https://www.gov.uk/government/publications/full-guidance-on-staying-at-home-and-away-from-others/full-guidance-on-staying-at-home-and-away-from-others.

22 World Health Organization (2021), op. cit.

23 Council of Europe, 'Respecting democracy, rule of law and human rights in the framework of the COVID-19 sanitary crisis: A toolkit for member states', 7 April 2020, SG/Inf(2020)11, 5.

> right to health and other human rights … Confinement measures are absolutely vital and necessary: with distressing reports of hospitals having to institute triage due to the saturation of their intensive care capacity, states must do all they can to slow the progression of the virus and everyone must do their part and uphold solidarity to this end.[24]

The commissioner also commented in April 2020 that, 'Persons with disabilities are not only often at increased risk of serious health complications, but they also have particular support needs in this challenging period'.[25]

In addition, it was recognised that individuals in detention facilities were at particular risk of contracting COVID-19 because of their circumstances of being confined in close proximity to large numbers of other persons.[26] Also, as was pointed out by HM Inspectorate of Prisons, adult prisoners tend to be at greater risk from COVID-19 due to pre-existing poor health, and the proportion of older prisoners has increased significantly during the past two decades.[27] As was stated by the Council of Europe Commissioner for Human Rights in April 2020,

> Convicted prisoners and persons on remand are among those most vulnerable to viral contagion as they are held in a high-risk environment: in general, detention facilities are not adapted to face large-scale epidemics, and the basic protective measures such as social distancing and hygiene

24 Council of Europe Commissioner for Human Rights, 'Older persons need more support than ever in the age of the Covid-19 pandemic', 20 March 2020, https://www.coe.int/en/web/commissioner/thematic-work/covid-19/-/asset_publisher/5cdZW0AJBMLl/content/older-persons-need-more-support-than-ever-in-the-age-of-the-covid-19-pandemic?inheritRedirect=false&redirect=https%3A%2F%2Fwww.coe.int%2Fen%2Fweb%2Fcommissioner%2Fthematic-work%2Fcovid-19%3Fp_p_id%3D101_INSTANCE_5cdZW0AJBMLl%26p_p_lifecycle%3D0%26p_p_state%3Dnormal%26p_p_mode%3Dview%26p_p_col_id%3Dcolumn-1%26p_p_col_count%3D1.

25 Council of Europe Commissioner for Human Rights, 'Persons with disabilities must not be left behind in the response to the COVID-19 pandemic', 2 April 2020, https://www.coe.int/en/web/commissioner/thematic-work/covid-19/-/asset_publisher/5cdZW0AJBMLl/content/persons-with-disabilities-must-not-be-left-behind-in-the-response-to-the-covid-19-pandemic?inheritRedirect=false&redirect=https%3A%2F%2Fwww.coe.int%2Fen%2Fweb%2Fcommissioner%2Fthematic-work%2Fcovid-19%3Fp_p_id%3D101_INSTANCE_5cdZW0AJBMLl%26p_p_lifecycle%3D0%26p_p_state%3Dnormal%26p_p_mode%3Dview%26p_p_col_id%3Dcolumn-1%26p_p_col_count%3D1.

26 World Health Organization, Regional Office for Europe, 'Preparedness, prevention and control of COVID-19 in prisons and other places of detention, interim guidance', 8 February 2021, https://www.who.int/europe/publications/i/item/WHO-EURO-2021-1405-41155-57257, at 1.

27 HM Inspectorate of Prisons, 'What happens to prisoners in a pandemic? A thematic review by HM Inspectorate of Prisons', February 2021, https://www.justiceinspectorates.gov.uk/hmiprisons/wp-content/uploads/sites/4/2021/02/What-happens-to-prisoners-in-a-pandemic.pdf, at para. 1.1.

> rules cannot be observed as easily as outside, exposing prisoners to greater health risks.[28]

In March 2020, the European Committee for the Prevention of Torture and Inhuman or Degrading Treatment or Punishment issued a statement of principles relating to the treatment of persons deprived of their liberty in the context of the COVID-19 pandemic, in which it emphasised that, 'The basic principle must be to take all possible action to protect the health and safety of all persons deprived of their liberty'. The statement proceeded to assert that,

> As regards the provision of health care, special attention will be required to the specific needs of detained persons with particular regard to vulnerable groups and/or at-risk groups, such as older persons and persons with pre-existing medical conditions. This includes, inter alia, screening for COVID-19 and pathways to intensive care as required.[29]

By July 2023, around 770,000,000 confirmed cases of COVID-19 worldwide have been reported to the World Health Organization, with around 7,000,000 deaths as a result of the virus.[30] The number of deaths would undoubtedly have been much higher if restrictive measures had not been implemented by states. As was stated by the World Health Organization on 14 June 2021, 'Public health and social measures (PHSM) have proven critical to limiting transmission of COVID-19 and reducing deaths'.[31]

Jurisprudence of the ECtHR on States' Duties to Provide Protection from COVID-19

Given the extent to which state responses to the pandemic engage human rights questions, it is unsurprising that such issues are now being raised before the ECtHR. As was noted in Chapter 1, these cases fall into two broad categories: cases in which applicants argue that states did not adopt sufficient

28 Council of Europe Commissioner for Human Rights, 'COVID-19 pandemic: Urgent steps are needed to protect the rights of prisoners in Europe', 6 April 2020, https://www.coe.int/en/web/commissioner/-/covid-19-pandemic-urgent-steps-are-needed-to-protect-the-rights-of-prisoners-in-europe.

29 European Committee for the Prevention of Torture and Inhuman or Degrading Treatment or Punishment, 'Statement of principles relating to the treatment of persons deprived of their liberty in the context of the coronavirus disease (Covid-19) pandemic', 20 March 2020, CPT/Inf(2020)13.

30 World Health Organization, 'WHO coronavirus (COVID-19) dashboard', https://covid19.who.int/.

31 World Health Organization, 'Considerations for implementing and adjusting public health and social measures in the context of COVID-19 – interim guidance', 14 June 2021, https://apps.who.int/iris/handle/10665/341811.

measures to protect them from COVID-19 and cases in which applicants claim that the measures which were taken themselves violated the ECHR. Cases falling within the first category are considered in this chapter, whilst cases falling within the second category are discussed in Chapters 3 and 4.

One of the earliest cases to come before the ECtHR involving issues relating to the COVID-19 pandemic was the admissibility decision of *Le Mailloux v France*.[32] In this case, the applicant argued that the state had not fulfilled its positive duties to protect the lives and physical integrity of individuals. Relying on Articles 2, 3, 8[33] and 10,[34] the applicant complained of restrictions on access to COVID-19 tests and to particular types of treatment as well as the interference in the private lives of people who died alone due to the virus. The ECtHR noted that states parties had positive obligations to adopt appropriate measures to safeguard the lives of individuals and to protect their physical integrity, including in relation to public health. However, the Court did not proceed to examine whether France had fulfilled its duties in this respect, as it deemed the application to be inadmissible. Essentially, the applicant had not demonstrated how he was affected personally by the state's response to the virus. The ECtHR pointed to Article 34 of the ECHR, under which, in order to have standing to take a case, an individual must show that they were 'directly affected' by the measure in question. However, the applicant had not provided any explanation of how any failures on the part of the state had affected his own health and private life. As the first admissibility decision in a case involving state responses to the pandemic, *Le Mailloux* provided a salutary warning to prospective applicants – if seeking to bring such a case before the ECtHR, an applicant must take care to explain how any alleged violations of the ECHR affected them at an individual level.

It is notable that in all the other cases to date in which arguments have been made that states did not take sufficient measures to protect individuals from the virus, the applicants have been detainees. This is somewhat unsurprising, given the particular vulnerability of this group, as discussed above. To date, there have been two judgments on the merits in such cases,[35] both of which were taken against Malta.

Feilazoo v Malta,[36] the judgment in which was issued on 11 March 2021, was a clear-cut case relating to the validity and conditions of the applicant's immigration detention in which the ECtHR found violations of Articles 3 and 5.[37] Various aspects of the applicant's detention were considered in the

32 App. No. 18108/20, decision of 5 November 2020.

33 Article 8 is the right to respect for private and family life.

34 Article 10 is the right to freedom of expression.

35 *Feilazoo v Malta*, App. No. 6865/19, judgment of 11 March 2021; and *Fenech v* Malta, App. No.19090/20, judgment of 1 March 2022.

36 App. No.6865/19, judgment of 11 March 2021.

37 Article 5 is the right to liberty and security of person.

Court's judgment, including a period of time during which he had been placed with newly arrived asylum seekers in COVID-19 quarantine. As there was no indication that such quarantine had been necessary for the applicant himself, the ECtHR was of the view that placing him with other persons who could have posed a risk to his health for several weeks did not comply with basic sanitary requirements and that there had, thus, been a breach of Article 3 due to the inadequate conditions of detention.

Under Article 46(2) of the ECHR, the execution of judgments of the ECtHR is supervised by the Committee of Ministers of the Council of Europe. This work is normally carried out at four meetings each year,[38] and the implementation by Malta of the judgment of the ECtHR in *Feilazoo* was assessed by the Committee of Ministers in September 2022. Action plans had been submitted by the state in December 2021 and June 2022. In these plans, it was explained that measures to address the breach of Article 3 included the introduction of a Close Monitoring Unit (CMU) with a view to providing separate accommodation for a range of persons including those with medical conditions which required them to be accommodated separately from others. Should an individual be suffering from an infectious disease, they would be required to reside in the CMU until they had received medical clearance to be permitted to join the general population in the compounds. In addition, COVID-19 preventative measures were enforced whereby all newly arrived migrants were required to undertake a period of mandatory quarantine to ensure that they tested negative for the virus. To avoid lengthy periods of quarantine, swab tests were carried out on the day of arrival and then seven days later in order to detect cases at as early a stage as possible. Residents had also been offered the COVID-19 vaccine, and 94% had taken up this offer. In response, the Committee of Ministers noted the ongoing efforts of the Maltese authorities to improve the living conditions in the detention centre in question and encouraged them to continue to pursue these efforts and to keep the committee informed thereof.[39]

In *Fenech v Malta*,[40] the judgment in which was issued on 1 March 2022, the applicant had been remanded in custody on suspicion of having been involved in a murder. He argued that there had been violations of Articles 2 and 3 on the grounds that sufficient measures had not been taken to protect him from contracting COVID-19 whilst in custody, particularly as he had only one kidney. In relation to the alleged breach of Article 2, the ECtHR was of the view that, in the context of the worldwide death toll as a result of COVID-19, it

38 For further information on this process, see Council of Europe, 'Supervision of execution of judgments of the European Court of Human Rights', https://www.coe.int/en/web/cm/execution-judgments.

39 *Feilazoo v Malta*, App. No. 6865/19, judgment of 11 March 2021, Examination of Committee of Ministers, 22 September 2022.

40 App. No. 19090/20, judgment of 1 March 2022.

could not consider that an individual was a victim of an alleged violation of Article 2 unless they had substantiated that in their own particular circumstances the acts or omissions of the state had or could have put their life at real and imminent risk. The Court noted that the applicant had not been infected by the virus and that vaccination had been made available to him by April 2021 at the latest. The ECtHR also noted that, apart from having only one kidney, the applicant had no underlying health conditions, and it had not been claimed that the absence of a kidney had affected his quality of life or required any treatment. The applicant had not relied on any studies which provided a clear picture of the chances that a man of his age lacking a kidney would certainly or quite likely die of COVID-19 were he to be infected. The Court could not, therefore, speculate on the question of whether the applicant's condition in the event of him contracting the virus would be of a life-threatening nature which would attract the applicability of Article 2. The ECtHR, thus, considered that the applicant could not claim to be a victim of the alleged breach of this provision. His complaint under Article 2 was, therefore, incompatible with the provisions of the ECHR and was rejected.

As regards the alleged breach of Article 3, the ECtHR commented that,

> given the nature of Covid-19, its well-documented effects, as well as the fact that it is easily transmitted from one person to another (via droplets or airborne particles containing the virus), the fears for the applicant's health in the eventuality of contracting the virus (were) not insignificant.[41]

The authorities, thus, had a duty to put in place particular measures aimed at avoiding infection, limiting the spread of COVID-19 once it reached the prison and providing sufficient medical care to those who contracted the virus. The Court, however, stated that,

> Preventive measures have to be proportionate to the risk at issue, however they should not pose an excessive burden on the authorities in view of the practical demands of imprisonment. This is even more so in the present case, where the authorities were confronted with a novel situation such as a global pandemic – unprecedented in recent decades – as a result of a new strain of coronavirus (called Covid-19) to which they had to react in a timely manner.[42]

The ECtHR noted that even prior to the first case of COVID-19 being detected in Malta, the prison authorities had already put in place a contingency plan in collaboration with the national health authorities. During the early stages of

41 At para. 129.
42 At para. 129.

the pandemic, the detention facility had effectively been in lockdown, with no visitors permitted and staff working weekly shifts to avoid excessive exposure to outside factors. Staff were provided with protective equipment, and disinfection by means of regular cleaning and use of hand sanitiser was in place. Also, physical distancing was possible given the size of the applicant's dormitory and the personal space available to him and the fact that he had access to open air all day long by means of a yard that was adjacent to his dormitory. There was no indication that the prison was overcrowded, and regular temperature checking of officials and inmates was conducted, with any suspected cases among inmates being immediately isolated. New detainees were subject to COVID-19 tests, the results of which determined where they would be placed. Between 1 September 2020 and 11 October 2021, any new detainee remained in quarantine for 14 days, and detainees who tested positive for COVID-19 or who were in quarantine underwent medical checks twice daily. More recently, the quarantine period had been decreased to 24–48 hours for those who tested negative. Also, by April 2021, all inmates had been given the opportunity to avail of vaccination.

In relation to the applicant's complaint that he was in need of protective measures beyond those provided to other detainees, the ECtHR commented that while procedures should be considered to allow prisoners at highest risk to be separated from others, the applicant had not made out a case that he fell within the category of the most vulnerable. The applicant did not submit that he was at any stage during his detention exposed to an individual who had COVID-19; however, even if he were to contract the virus, there was no indication that qualified medical assistance would not be available. Also, the mere fact that a group of detainees (none of whom were known to have COVID-19) shared a dormitory and used the same medical, catering and other facilities did not in itself raise an issue under Article 3. By contrast, the applicant in *Feilazoo*, who had not been in need of quarantine, had been placed in quarantine quarters with individuals who could have posed a risk to his health. The ECtHR, thus, considered that the authorities in *Fenech* had put in place adequate and proportionate measures to prevent and limit the spread of the COVID-19 virus, and there had, therefore, been no breach of Article 3 in this respect.

One further decision has been taken by the ECtHR in a case involving arguments that the state in question did not take sufficient measures to protect the applicant from the virus. In the admissibility decision in *Ünsal and Timtik v Turkey*,[43] the applicants were lawyers who had been detained on suspicion of being members of a terrorist organisation. In March 2019, they had then been found guilty and sentenced to terms of imprisonment of 10 years and six months and 13 years and six months, respectively. In early 2020, they had

43 App. No. 36331/20, decision of 8 June 2021.

begun a hunger strike to protest against *inter alia* the criminal proceedings against them. In July 2020, the applicants had requested their release; however, this request was refused, and they were transferred to hospital. Relying on Articles 2, 3 and 5 of the ECHR, the applicants complained of being held in detention, alleging that the hospitals in which they had been held were dedicated to COVID-19 pandemic treatments, despite the fact that they considered themselves to be at risk due to their fragile state of health caused by their hunger strike. However, according to information provided by the Turkish government, the hospital in which the first applicant had been kept had five buildings, only one of which was dedicated to COVID-19 treatment, and, likewise, the hospital in which the second applicant had been kept was not dedicated to the treatment of COVID-19. The ECtHR was of the view that there was no element which supported the allegation of a specific risk of infection, taking into account measures which had been in place, such as disinfection, mask wearing and social distancing, with regard to health officers and visitors. This was not a situation in which additional measures were needed for the medical care or treatment of the detainees, and the ECtHR found that the application was inadmissible because it was manifestly ill-founded.[44]

There are currently a sizeable number of pending applications to the ECtHR involving issues regarding the responses of states to the COVID-19 pandemic. A significant proportion of these concern conditions of detention. These cases relate to specific and limited circumstances in which the applicants are arguing that the states in question did not provide them with sufficient protection from the COVID-19 virus. For example, *Hafeez v the United Kingdom*[45] concerns the risk of life imprisonment without parole and inadequate conditions of detention due to the COVID-19 pandemic in a case relating to the extradition to the United States of a 60-year-old man with a number of health conditions, which include diabetes and asthma. *Maratsis and Others v Greece*[46] and *Vasilakis and Others v Greece*[47] concern the conditions of detention of HIV-positive prisoners and, in particular, raise the issue of whether the authorities took adequate steps to protect the health of the applicants, as persons living with HIV, in the context of the pandemic. *Vlamis and Others v Greece*[48] also concerns the applicants' conditions of detention, and the applicants complain, in particular, about the lack of protective measures against the propagation of the COVID-19 virus. In *Rus v Romania*[49] the applicant complains that he was infected with the COVID-19 virus while in prison and that this was due to

44 Under Article 35(3)(a) of the ECHR, the ECtHR shall declare inadmissible any application if it considers that the application is manifestly ill-founded.

45 App. No. 14198/20.

46 App. No. 39335/20.

47 App. No. 30379/20.

48 App. Nos. 29655/20, 29689/20, 30240/20, 30418/20 and 30574/20.

49 App. No. 2621/21.

the condition of his detention, in particular the overcrowding. *Riela v Italy*[50] concerns the alleged incompatibility of the applicant's state of health with his continued detention. The applicant complains of the absence of adequate medical treatment for his multiple diseases and that the authorities had not protected him from the risk of contracting COVID-19. *Faia v Italy*[51] concerns the alleged incompatibility of the applicant's medical condition and serious disability with detention in a correctional facility. The applicant also complains that the measures put in place by the authorities to protect him from the risk of contracting COVID-19 were inadequate. *Krstic v Serbia*[52] concerns pending extradition proceedings of the nine applicants from Serbia to Texas in the United States. The applicants submit *inter alia* that, if extradited, they would be subjected to inhuman or degrading treatment as a result of exposure to severe conditions of detention, particularly taking into account the number of COVID-19 infected people among inmates and in Texas more generally.

Conclusion

In conclusion, at the onset of the pandemic it was imperative for states to adopt measures to protect their citizens from the deadly COVID-19 virus. Failure to do so risked violating the rights of such citizens under Articles 2 and 3 of the ECHR. The duties of states to adopt protective measures were especially pertinent in respect of persons who were clinically vulnerable to the virus, such as those who were elderly or who had underlying health conditions. States also had particular duties to ensure that the rights of other individuals who were at greater risk of contracting COVID-19, such as those in detention facilities, were not breached in the context of the pandemic. Indeed, it can be seen that almost all of the cases in which applicants argue that states have not adopted sufficient protective measures against COVID-19 involve conditions of detention. This is not surprising, given the particular vulnerability of detainees during the pandemic, as discussed earlier in the chapter. Such cases tend to relate to particular circumstances in certain facilities and are, therefore, of very specific application.

However, as was discussed in Chapter 1, there is a second category of ECHR claims in the context of the pandemic. Rather than involving arguments that states did not put in place sufficient measures to protect individuals from the virus, this category of cases entails arguments that the measures put in place to this end themselves involved breaches of rights. As will be discussed in Chapter 3, in particular, and also in Chapter 4, such cases tend to be somewhat more problematic. In these instances, applicants argue that general

50 App. No. 17378/20.
51 App. No.17378/20.
52 App. No. 35246/21.

measures adopted by states during the early months of the pandemic to prevent the spread of the virus were in breach of the ECHR. It is certainly not disputed that such measures had an enormous impact on the lives of individuals and caused considerable amounts of suffering. Such measures involved very substantial limitations on the rights of individuals under provisions, such as the right to respect for private and family life under Article 8; the right to freedom of thought, conscience and religion under Article 9; the right to freedom of expression under Article 10; the right to freedom of assembly and association under Article 11; and the right to freedom of movement under Article 2 of Protocol No. 4. However, it must be remembered that, in the circumstances of a global pandemic, unprecedented in living memory, states were taking measures to protect the lives of their citizens from a deadly new virus about which little was known, against which there was no vaccine and for which very few treatments were available. As will be discussed, it is submitted that this is an area in which a wide margin of appreciation should be afforded to states. It will be argued that, in order to preserve the legitimacy of human rights law, the ECtHR must strike the correct balance between holding states to account for clear violations of the ECHR – as it quite rightly did in *Feilazoo* – but also being cautious of finding breaches in cases involving public restrictions which were applied for the purpose of protecting life and health in response to a global pandemic.

As will be discussed in Chapter 3, generally one of the most prominent aspects of the responses of states to the pandemic was to put in place measures prohibiting or restricting public gatherings. Such measures raise issues in relation to the right to freedom of assembly and association under Article 11 of the ECHR; the right to freedom of expression under Article 10, in the case of public gatherings for the purpose of peaceful protest; and the right to freedom of thought, conscience and religion under Article 9, in the case of gatherings for collective worship. However, the measures adopted by states because of the pandemic were not, of course, limited to restrictions on public gatherings; rather, they impacted upon the lives of individuals in a wide range of other ways which also engage various provisions of the ECHR and in relation to which issues have also been raised before the ECtHR, as will be discussed in Chapter 4.

3 The ECHR and Restrictions on Public Gatherings

In contrast to Chapter 2, which focused on the duties of the state to provide protection from COVID-19, Chapters 3 and 4 now turn to the human rights implications of the measures which were put in place to this end. As was discussed in Chapter 2, at the onset of the pandemic, it was imperative for states to adopt measures to protect their citizens from the deadly COVID-19 virus, and failure to do so would have risked breaching the rights of such citizens under Article 2 (the right to life) and Article 3 (the right to be free from torture or inhuman or degrading treatment) of the ECHR. However, conversely, the protective measures which were put in place themselves raised human rights issues, and cases are bring brought to the ECtHR in which applicants argue that measures put in place by states entailed violations of their rights under the ECHR. As is discussed in this chapter, such cases tend to be somewhat more problematic than those which were considered in Chapter 2. It is certainly not disputed that measures put in place by states, particularly during the early stages of the pandemic, had a huge impact on the lives of individuals and frequently resulted in considerable levels of suffering. For example, the mental health of many people was greatly affected,[1] and many lost their businesses or their employment.[2] Such measures certainly involved considerable limitations on the rights of individuals under provisions of the ECHR, such as the right to respect for private and family life under Article 8; the right to freedom of thought, conscience and religion under Article 9; the right to freedom of expression under Article 10; the right to freedom of assembly and association under Article 11; and the right to freedom of movement under Article 2 of Protocol No. 4.

In the normal course of events, such restrictions would certainly have amounted to very clear violations of such provisions. However, the pandemic gave rise to truly extraordinary circumstances. Never before in living

1 Mental Health Foundation, 'Mental health in the COVID-19 pandemic: Recommendations for prevention', https://www.mentalhealth.org.uk/coronavirus/pandemic-recommendations-prevention.

2 International Labour Organization, 'COVID-19 and the world of work', https://www.ilo.org/global/topics/coronavirus/lang--en/index.htm.

DOI: 10.4324/9781003383437-3

memory had a deadly virus swept around the globe in such a manner. In such a rapidly developing situation, states had to act quickly, with little time for in-depth reflection. This was a deadly new virus about which little was known at the time and for which there was no vaccine. In such circumstances, the only real option for governments was to adopt measures which strictly limited contact. Simply put, in the absence of contact, a virus cannot spread. A key duty of states is to protect the lives of their citizens, and it must be remembered that the restrictions were put in place to this end. It is, therefore, argued in this chapter that this is an area in which a wide margin of appreciation should be afforded to states. Essentially, it is submitted that the ECtHR must be cautious of finding violations in cases involving public restrictions which were applied for the purpose of protecting life and health in response to a global pandemic, not least as such findings could open the floodgates to a considerable number of cases coming before the Court involving similar measures in many other states.[3] As was noted in Chapter 2, in April 2020, half of the world's population were in lockdown.[4] Whilst the floodgates argument in itself is not a sufficient reason to refrain from finding a breach of the ECHR, the difficulty is that if the concept of a human rights violation is defined too broadly, the seriousness of such a breach is diluted. Taken to the extreme, if everything is a human rights violation, then nothing is. In order to preserve the legitimacy of human rights law, the ECtHR must strike the correct balance between holding states to account for clear violations of the ECHR, as it quite correctly did in *Feilazoo v Malta*,[5] as was discussed in Chapter 2, but also being cautious of finding breaches in cases involving public restrictions imposed to protect lives.

Generally, one of the most prominent aspects of the responses of states to the pandemic was to put in place measures prohibiting or restricting public gatherings, and it is on this aspect that Chapter 3 focuses. Such measures raise issues in relation to the right to freedom of assembly and association under Article 11 of the ECHR, as well as the right to freedom of expression under Article 10, in the case of public gatherings for the purpose of peaceful protest, and the right to freedom of religion under Article 9, in the case of gatherings for collective worship. A prohibition of public gatherings due to the pandemic was the subject of *Communauté Genevoise D'Action Syndicale*

3 It should be noted however that under Article 35(1) of the ECHR, the ECtHR may only deal with a matter 'after all domestic remedies have been exhausted, according to the generally recognised rules of international law, and within a period of four months from the date on which the final decision was taken'.

4 Euronews, 'Coronavirus: Half of humanity now on lockdown as 90 countries call for confinement', 3 April 2020, https://www.euronews.com/2020/04/02/coronavirus-in-europe-spain-s-death-toll-hits-10-000-after-record-950-new-deaths-in-24-hou.

5 App. No. 6865/19, judgment of 11 March 2021.

(CGAS) v Switzerland,[6] a case in which the ECtHR issued an important judgment on 15 March 2022, and which is considered in detail in this chapter. In this case, the applicant, an association with the aim of defending the interests of workers and trade unions, argued that the prohibition in question breached Article 11. The ECtHR held that the interference with the rights protected by Article 11 had not been proportionate to the aims pursued and that there had, thus, been a violation of this provision. The decision, however, was not unanimous, and it is argued that the approach of the dissenting judges was, in fact, correct. There are currently a number of applications pending before the ECtHR which raise similar issues to those considered in *CGAS*, as is also discussed in this chapter.[7] In addition, prior to the judgment of the ECtHR in *CGAS*, the compatibility with Article 11 of restrictions on public gatherings in the context of the pandemic had been considered by the domestic courts in the UK. Interestingly, in *R (Dolan) v Secretary of State for Health and Social Care*,[8] in considering the compatibility with Article 11 of arguably more stringent measures than those at issue in *CGAS*, the UK courts adopted a position which was diametrically opposed to the approach later taken by the ECtHR in the *CGAS* case. The chapter argues that the approach of the UK courts in *Dolan* seems to have more to commend it than that of the ECtHR in *CGAS*.

The restrictions on public gatherings which many states imposed in response to the pandemic often included prohibitions on gatherings for collective worship. The inability to gather together for worship was very difficult for many people, and questions surrounding the compatibility of such restrictions with the ECHR have been raised before the ECtHR in a number of pending applications.[9] Although the ECtHR has not yet made a ruling on the compatibility with Article 9 on general prohibitions on gatherings for collective worship in the context of the pandemic, it is noteworthy that questions surrounding the extent to which the forced closure of places of worship in Scotland due to the pandemic was compatible with Article 9 have been considered by the Court of Session of Scotland in the case of *Philip and Others for Judicial Review of the closure of places of worship in Scotland*,[10] as is also discussed in this chapter.

6 App. No. 21881/20, judgment of 15 March 2022.

7 *Central Unitaria de Traballadores/as v Spain*, App. No. 49363/20; *Jarocki v Poland*, App. No. 39750/20; *Nemytov v Russia*, App. No. 1257/21; *Azar v* Russia, App. No. 3244/21; and *Kostyukhin v Russia*, App. No. 24699/21.

8 [2020] EWHC 1786 (Admin); [2020] EWCA Civ 1605.

9 *Association of orthodox Ecclesiastical Obedience v Greece*, App. No. 52104/20; *Megard v France*, App. No. 32647/22; and *Figel' v Slovakia*, App. No. 12131/21.

10 [2021] CSOH 32, paras. 95–127. For further discussion of this case, see Greene, A., 'Closing places of worship and COVID-19: Towards a culture of justification? (2021) 25 *Edinburgh Law Review* 393.

Article 11 in a Pandemic Context

Article 11(1) of the ECHR states that, 'Everyone has the right to freedom of peaceful assembly and to freedom of association with others, including the right to form and to join trade unions for the protection of his interests'. However, under Article 11(2),

> No restrictions shall be placed on the exercise of these rights other than such as are prescribed by law and are necessary in a democratic society in the interests of national security or public safety, for the prevention of disorder or crime, for the protection of health or morals or for the protection of the rights and freedoms of others.

It is abundantly clear that the measures imposed by states in response to the COVID-19 pandemic constituted a severe limitation on the right to freedom of association with others. Indeed, preventing individuals, as much as possible, from engaging in 'association with others', beyond those in their own households, was the key point of the lockdown measures which were adopted by many states. In the case of public gatherings for the purpose of peaceful protest, the right to freedom of expression under Article 10 may also have been restricted, and a similar limitation clause to that found in Article 11(2) is also contained in Article 10(2).[11] As noted in Chapter 1, issues surrounding measures adopted by states parties due to the pandemic and their compliance with the ECHR do not hinge on the question of whether they restricted rights such as the right to freedom of association – they undoubtedly did – but, rather, they relate to the question of whether the restrictions were legitimate for the purposes of protecting health and protecting the rights and freedoms of others. In a toolkit for member states on 'Respecting democracy, rule of law and human rights in the framework of the COVID-19 sanitary crisis' which was issued by the Council of Europe in April 2020, it was stated that,

> Effective enjoyment of all these rights and freedoms guaranteed by Articles 8, 9, 10 and 11 of the Convention is a benchmark of modern democratic societies. Restrictions on them are only permissible if they are established by law and proportionate to the legitimate aim pursued, including the protection of health. The significant restrictions to usual social activities,

11 Article 10(2) states that, 'The exercise of these freedoms, since it carries with it duties and responsibilities, may be subject to such formalities, conditions, restrictions or penalties as are prescribed by law and are necessary in a democratic society, in the interests of national security, territorial integrity or public safety, for the prevention of disorder or crime, for the protection of health or morals, for the protection of the reputation or rights of others, for preventing the disclosure of information received in confidence, or for maintaining the authority and impartiality of the judiciary'.

> including access to public places of worship, public gatherings and wedding and funeral ceremonies, may inevitably lead to arguable complaints under the above provisions. It is for the authorities to ensure that any such restriction, whether or not it is based on a derogation, is clearly established by law, in compliance with relevant constitutional guarantees and proportionate to the aim it pursues. While heightened restrictions to the above-mentioned rights may be fully justified in time of crisis, harsh criminal sanctions give rise to concern and must be subject to a strict scrutiny.[12]

In order to protect the right to life under Article 2 and the right to be free from torture or inhuman or degrading treatment under Article 3 – rights which, as was discussed in Chapter 2, were being threatened by the COVID-19 virus – it was necessary to severely restrict the right to freedom of association under Article 11. It has always been accepted that the application of human rights standards frequently involves a balancing exercise, and nowhere is this more apparent than with the application of ECHR provisions in the context of the pandemic. As McColgan states, 'Rights do not exist in a vacuum, but have to be balanced against other rights'.[13] Although, technically, there is no hierarchy of rights as such, Articles 2 and 3 of the ECHR are not subject to a limitation clause such as that found in Article 11(2). Article 2(1) states that, 'Everyone's right to life shall be protected by law'. In comparison with the somewhat broad limitation clause contained in Article 11(2), Article 2 simply proceeds to set out very specific circumstances in which deprivation of life will not be regarded as being inflicted in contravention of the right to life. These are 'in the execution of a sentence of a court following conviction of a crime for which this penalty is provided by law',[14] or when the deprivation of life

> results from the use of force which is no more than absolutely necessary: (a) in defence of any person from unlawful violence; (b) in order to effect a lawful arrest or to prevent the escape of a person lawfully detained; (c) in action lawfully taken for the purpose of quelling a riot or insurrection.[15]

Article 3 is expressed in even more stark terms, simply stating that, 'No one shall be subjected to torture or to inhuman or degrading treatment or punishment'; therefore, in a sense, Articles 2 and 3 cannot be balanced against other rights such as Article 11. Rather, it is the case that if the rights contained

12 Council of Europe, 'Respecting democracy, rule of law and human rights in the framework of the COVID-19 sanitary crisis: A toolkit for member states', 7 April 2020, SG/Inf(2020)11, 6.

13 McColgan, A., 'Women and the Human Rights Act' (2000) 51 *Northern Ireland Legal Quarterly* 417 at 444.

14 Article 2(1).

15 Article 2(2).

in Articles 2 and 3 come into conflict with other rights, the rights found in Articles 2 and 3 must prevail. It is submitted, therefore, that the ECtHR must be cautious of finding violations of provisions such as Article 11 in respect of measures which were adopted with the aim of protecting life in the context of the COVID-19 pandemic.

Importantly, the ECtHR has established that should an applicant wish to complain of a violation of their rights under provisions such as Article 11, in order to demonstrate the victim status necessary under Article 34 to bring a case, 'they must produce reasonable and convincing evidence of the likelihood that a violation affecting them personally will occur; mere suspicion or conjecture is insufficient in this respect'.[16] In *Magdic v Croatia*[17] (which is further discussed in Chapter 4), the applicant complained about measures which had been in place from 19 March 2020 until 11 May 2020 in order to contain the spread of the COVID-19 virus which prohibited all public events and gatherings of more than five persons in one place as well as suspended the work of all shops except those which were essential, such as pharmacies and grocery stores. Religious gatherings were also suspended. From 23 March 2020, a further measure had been put in place whereby people were not permitted to leave their territorial unit (that is, their county) except for justified reasons such as travelling for work which could not be done from home or taking care of a family member. The applicant argued that these measures had breached his right to freedom of assembly under Article 11, his right to freedom of religion under Article 9 and his right to freedom of movement under Article 2 of Protocol No. 4. However, in deeming the application to be inadmissible, the ECtHR commented that the applicant had not provided any information regarding his personal situation beyond his identity and his occupation. He had provided no information to demonstrate how precisely the measures in question affected or would be likely to affect him directly or target him due to his possible individual characteristics. For example, whilst alleging a violation of his freedom of assembly, the applicant had not specified which public gatherings he could not attend due to the measures in question. The ECtHR could not, therefore, conduct an individual assessment of the applicant's situation and stated that, 'It thus appears that the applicant wishes to complain about the impugned measures in a general manner, contemplating that, as a result of their adoption, his freedoms were automatically violated'.[18] The Court was of the view that the applicant could not be regarded as a victim

16 *Magdic v Croatia*, App. No. 17578/20, decision of 5 July 2022, at para. 9. Article 34 states that, 'The Court may receive applications from any person, nongovernmental organisation or group of individuals claiming to be the victim of a violation by one of the High Contracting Parties of the rights set forth in the Convention or the Protocols thereto. The High Contracting Parties undertake not to hinder in any way the effective exercise of this right'.

17 App. No. 17578/20, decision of 5 July 2022.

18 At para. 11.

for the purposes of Article 34 of the ECHR, and, therefore, the application was incompatible with the provisions of the Convention within the meaning of Article 35(3)(a)[19] and must be rejected. As in *Le Mailloux v France*[20] (which was discussed in Chapter 2), the admissibility decision in *Magdic v Croatia* again serves to emphasise that if seeking to bring a complaint before the ECtHR regarding state responses to the COVID-19 pandemic, an applicant must take care to explain how any alleged violations of the ECHR affected them at an individual level. Under Article 34, in order to have standing to take a case, an individual must show that they were 'directly affected' by the measure in question.

As was discussed in Chapter 1, Article 15(1) of the ECHR permits states 'in time of war or other public emergency threatening the life of the nation' to adopt measures derogating from their duties under the Convention 'to the extent strictly required by the exigencies of the situation', provided that such measures are not inconsistent with the state's other duties under international law.[21] Under Article 15(2), derogations are not permitted from Article 2 (except as regards deaths resulting from lawful acts of war), Article 3, the prohibition of slavery under Article 4(1), or Article 7, which provides that no one shall be held guilty of any criminal offence on account of any act or omission which did not constitute a criminal offence at the time when it was committed. Again, the vital importance accorded to Articles 2 and 3 is seen in the fact that the rights contained therein are non-derogable. However, derogations from other provisions, such as Article 11, are permissible, provided that the criteria set out in Article 15(1) are met. Notably, in March/April 2020, ten states chose to enter derogations in respect of the measures which they were adopting due to the pandemic.[22] All of these states referred *inter alia* to Article 11 in their derogation notifications, apart from Armenia, Romania and San Marino, all of which submitted more general derogation notifications which did not specify particular provisions of the ECHR.

Nevertheless, the large majority of the states parties to the ECHR chose not to enter derogations in relation to the measures which they took in response to COVID-19. It would, of course, have been abundantly clear to such states that such measures constituted very extensive limitations on the right to freedom of association under Article 11 as well as on other rights. The reasons

19 Under Article 35(3)(a), the ECtHR shall declare inadmissible any individual application if it considers that 'the application is incompatible with the provisions of the Convention or the Protocols thereto, manifestly ill-founded, or an abuse of the right of individual application'.

20 App. No. 18108/20, decision of 5 November 2020.

21 For discussion generally of the use of derogations from the ECHR, see Wallace, S., 'Derogations from the European Convention on Human Rights: The case for reform' (2020) 20 *Human Rights Law Review* 769.

22 Albania, Armenia, Estonia, Georgia, Latvia, North Macedonia, the Republic of Moldova, Romania, San Marino and Serbia. The notifications under Article 15 in the context of the COVID-19 pandemic are available at https://www.coe.int/en/web/conventions/derogations-covid-19.

why the majority of states parties did not enter derogations in respect of such measures, whilst ten states did, are not immediately apparent. A geographical trend, to some extent, can be observed in that all the states which entered derogations, with the exception of San Marino, are eastern European states. There may perhaps have been an element of states following the lead of those in geographical proximity. Alternatively, it is possible that many states, suddenly finding themselves in the midst of an unprecedented crisis which was developing at an alarming rate, were focused on seemingly more immediate issues such as protecting lives rather than on the question of whether it was necessary to derogate from a human rights treaty. Although it appears that the states which did not enter derogations chose to rely on clauses such as that found in Article 11(2), for many states, this may not actually have been a conscious decision. The question of derogation may not have occurred to some, and others may simply have assumed that, as measures limiting contact as far as possible seemed to be the only available option to try to limit the spread of the virus, no issues would arise as regards compliance with the ECHR.[23]

However, as was considered in Chapter 1, it is by no means clear where the line is drawn between a permissible restriction under a limitation clause, such as that contained in Article 11(2), and a situation which would necessitate a derogation. In the toolkit issued by the Council of Europe in April 2020, it was stated that,

> While some restrictive measures adopted by member states may be justified on the ground of the usual provisions of the [ECHR] relating to the protection of health … measures of exceptional nature may require derogations from the states' obligations under the Convention. It is for each state to assess whether the measures it adopts warrant such a derogation, depending on the nature and extent of restrictions applied to the rights and freedoms protected by the Convention.[24]

This statement does not, however, seem to clarify the question of which types of measures would require a derogation and which would not. Nevertheless,

23 For discussion from early in the pandemic of whether derogations from the ECHR were necessary, see Dzehtsiarou, K., 'Article 15 derogations: Are they really necessary during the COVID-19 pandemic?'(2020) *European Human Rights Law Review* 359; Greene, A., 'On the value of derogations from the European Convention on Human Rights in response to the COVID-19 pandemic: A rejoinder' (2020) *European Human Rights Law Review* 526; and Hickman, T., 'The coronavirus pandemic and derogation from the European Convention on Human Rights' (2020) *European Human Rights Law Review* 593. For discussion of derogations from the International Covenant on Civil and Political Rights in the context of the pandemic, see Qiu, D., 'Human rights protection under the ICCPR: When can and should states derogate? A critical analysis in the context of New Zealand's COVID-19 response' (2022) *International Journal of Human Rights*, DOI: 10.1080/13642987.2022.2066080.

24 Council of Europe, op. cit., at 2.

the toolkit indicates that although derogations are assessed by the ECtHR in any relevant cases brought before it, the Court grants states a large margin of appreciation in this regard.[25] As the ECtHR stated in *Ireland v United Kingdom*,

> It falls in the first place to each Contracting State, with its responsibility for 'the life of [its] nation', to determine whether that life is threatened by a 'public emergency' and, if so, how far it is necessary to go in attempting to overcome the emergency. By reason of their direct and continuous contact with the pressing needs of the moment, the national authorities are in principle in a better position than the international judge to decide both on the presence of such an emergency and on the nature and scope of derogations necessary to avert it.[26]

It appears, therefore, that when assessing measures adopted by states in response to the pandemic, the ECtHR may afford a wider margin of appreciation to states which entered derogations than to those which did not. In retrospect, it seems that states may have been well advised to enter derogations as seen from the judgment in *Communauté Genevoise D'Action Syndicale (CGAS) v Switzerland.*

Communauté Genevoise D'Action Syndicale (CGAS) v Switzerland

The judgment of the ECtHR in *Communauté Genevoise D'Action Syndicale (CGAS) v Switzerland*[27] was issued on 15 March 2022. The applicant in this case was an association which had the aim of defending the interests of workers and of its member organisations, particularly in relation to trade union and democratic freedoms. As such, the association generally organised and participated in large numbers of events each year in the Canton of Geneva. However, due to an ordinance enacted by the Federal Council in response to the pandemic, public and private events were prohibited from 16 March 2020. Failing to comply with this prohibition could have resulted in a fine or a custodial sentence of up to three years. The rule was relaxed in May 2020, allowing for gatherings of up to 30 participants. In June 2020, the ban on public events was lifted, although events involving in excess of 1,000 participants remained prohibited until August 2020. The applicant complained that

25 Council of Europe, op. cit., at 2.

26 App. No. 5310/71, judgment of 18 January 1978, at para. 207.

27 App. No. 21881/20, judgment of 15 March 2022. Discussion of this case can also be found in McQuigg, R., 'Responding to a crisis: The European Court of Human Rights and the COVID-19 pandemic' (2022) *European Human Rights Law Review* 283.

due to the ordinance in question it had had to cancel a rally which had been planned for 1 May 2020, and that it had, therefore, been deprived of the right to organise and participate in public events. The prohibition of public gatherings undoubtedly constituted a restriction on the applicant's right to freedom of assembly under Article 11 of the ECHR. The question which fell to be considered by the ECtHR was whether this interference was justified on the grounds of protecting health and the rights and freedoms of others.

In its judgment, the Court noted the very serious threat to public health which had been posed by COVID-19. Very little had been known about the virus at the start of the pandemic, so the state had had to react quickly during the period of time under consideration. The ECtHR also noted the competing interests at stake, in particular the positive duty on the part of the state to protect the lives and health of the persons within its jurisdiction. However, the Court was of the view that the outright prohibition of a certain type of conduct was a drastic measure which required strong reasons to justify it, and no scrutiny had been carried out by the domestic courts. In relation to the penalties for failing to comply with the prohibition on public events, the ECtHR expressed the opinion that these were very severe and were liable to have a chilling effect on potential participants. The Court also referred to the fact that Switzerland had not entered a derogation under Article 15 of the ECHR and, therefore, had been obliged to comply fully with Article 11 within the margin of appreciation afforded to it. The ECtHR held that, in light of the importance of freedom of peaceful assembly in a democratic society and, in particular, of the values promoted by the applicant, the blanket nature and significant length of the ban on public events and the nature and severity of the potential penalties, the interference with the rights protected by Article 11 had not been proportionate to the aims pursued. Also, the domestic courts had not conducted a review of the measures in question during the relevant period. The Court was, thus, of the view that the state had gone beyond the margin of appreciation afforded to it, the interference had not been necessary in a democratic society and there had, therefore, been a violation of Article 11.

The Court's decision in *CGAS* is arguably problematic. The three dissenting judges in the case pointed to the judgment in *Vavřička and Others v. Czech Republic*,[28] in which the Grand Chamber stated that principle matters of public health fall within the margin of appreciation of states and asserted that 'the margin of appreciation available to the respondent State is generally wide when it has to strike a balance between competing private and public interests or different rights protected by the Convention'.[29] The dissenting judges in

28 App. Nos. 47621/13, 3867/14, 73094/14, 19298/15, 19306/15 and 43883/15, judgment of 8 April 2021.

29 *Vavřička*, at para. 275.

CGAS were of the view that the majority judgment deprived of substance the conclusion of the Grand Chamber's judgment in *Vavřička*. Although the facts of *Vavřička* did not relate to the COVID-19 pandemic, it was held, in this case, that imposing fines on parents and excluding children from preschool due to refusal to comply with a statutory child vaccination duty fell within the state's margin of appreciation and, therefore, did not constitute a violation of the right to respect for private and family life under Article 8, the right to freedom of opinion under Article 9 or the right to education under Article 2 of Protocol No. 1. It seems that the measure in question in *Vavřička* was more intrusive than that which was at issue in *CGAS*, and the dissenting judges in the latter saw no reason why a limitation on freedom of assembly under Article 11 would not fall within the same margin of appreciation.

It has been established by the ECtHR that when there is no consensus among states parties, a wider margin of appreciation should be afforded.[30] There is certainly no consensus among states parties against the type of measure in question in *CGAS* – any consensus was actually in favour of this type of measure, given that it appears to have been very much in line with those imposed by many other states in Europe and beyond. For example, during April 2020, almost half of the world's population were in lockdown.[31] By contrast, the measure at issue in *Vavřička* was not of a type that is widely applied among states, yet it was deemed to fall within the state's margin of appreciation. It is submitted that the issue raised in *CGAS* is a paradigm example of a situation in which a wide margin of appreciation should be granted to the state.

In addition, it must be remembered that during the time period in question in *CGAS*, vaccines against the COVID-19 virus were not yet available. In the absence of a vaccine, the most effective way of preventing the spread of a contagious virus is simply to keep people apart as much as possible. As stated by the World Health Organization, 'Current evidence suggests that the (COVID-19) virus spreads mainly between people who are in close contact with each other'.[32] A strong argument could, therefore, be made that the measure in question in *CGAS* was actually a reasonable and logical response on the part of the state which was adopted to protect the lives not only of those who may otherwise have participated in large public gatherings but also of individuals

30 As was stated by the Grand Chamber in *Dickson v the United Kingdom*, 'Where … there is no consensus within the member States of the Council of Europe either as to the relative importance of the interest at stake or as to how best to protect it, the margin will be wider'. (App. No. 44362/04, judgment of 4 December 2007, at para. 78).

31 Euronews, op. cit.

32 World Health Organization, 'Coronavirus disease (COVID-19): How is it transmitted?', 23 December 2021, https://www.who.int/emergencies/diseases/novel-coronavirus-2019/question-and-answers-hub/q-a-detail/coronavirus-disease-covid-19-how-is-it-transmitted.

within the wider community who may not have attended but to whom the virus may have subsequently spread.

Also, although the ECtHR was of the view that the time period during which the ban on public events was in place was significant, it could be argued that the period in question was actually very short, particularly in the context of a global pandemic which has now been continuing for almost four years. After around only two months of the ban being put in place, gatherings of up to 30 people had been permitted, and the ban was then lifted the following month for events involving up to 1,000 participants. It is arguable that the measure, therefore, constituted a proportionate response to a very serious crisis and one which was relaxed in stages as soon as was permitted by the ongoing public health emergency. It could also be argued that the rolling adjustments were reflective of the state taking steps – in the face of constantly new information regarding the best way to address the virus – to ensure that restrictions were proportionate. Moreover, although the ECtHR was of the view that the penalties for failing to comply with the prohibition on public events were liable to have a chilling effect on potential participants, the very purpose of having penalties was to deter participation in such events, and they, therefore, needed to be sufficiently strong in order to do so.

The ECtHR made the point in *CGAS* that the Swiss courts had not conducted a review of the measures in question during the relevant period; however, it is very likely that similar measures were not reviewed by the courts in various other Council of Europe states in which they had been imposed. Indeed, the dissenting judges noted a decision of 18 August 2020 of the administrative chamber of the Court of Justice of the Canton of Geneva in which it was held that the ordinance in question did not violate a higher standard. Although this judgment was delivered after the date on which the applicant's planned rally had been due to take place, the dissenting judges pointed to the fact that it is up to the organiser of an event to request authorisation in sufficient time to allow a reasoned decision to be made and, in the event of refusal, for the courts to examine any appeal without undue time pressure. The dissenting judges were of the view that the applicant could have informed the authorities of its intention to hold a rally on 1 May 2020 well before this date, thus allowing for a decision to be made in good time and for a domestic court to rule on the compatibility of the decision with the provisions of the ECHR.

Whilst it is arguable that if the ECtHR had had evidence of the domestic courts carefully considering the proportionality of the measure, it may well have deferred to the state authority's assessment of proportionality, it is, nevertheless, possible that, should the ECtHR's finding of a violation in *CGAS* be upheld by the Grand Chamber,[33] this could open the floodgates to a substantial number of cases coming before the Court involving similar measures in many

33 The case was referred to the Grand Chamber on 5 September 2022.

other states.[34] Whilst the floodgates argument in itself is not a sufficient reason to hold back from finding a breach of the ECHR, the difficulty is that if the concept of a human rights violation is defined too broadly, this dilutes the seriousness of such a breach. Taken to the extreme, if everything is a human rights violation, then nothing is. In order to preserve the legitimacy of human rights law, the ECtHR must strike the correct balance between holding states to account for clear breaches of the ECHR, as it quite correctly did in *Feilazoo v Malta*[35] (as was discussed in Chapter 2) but also being cautious of finding violations in cases involving public restrictions which were applied for the purpose of protecting life and health in response to a global pandemic.

When assessing measures adopted by states due to the pandemic, the decision of the ECtHR in *CGAS* seems to indicate that a more restrictive approach may be taken by the Court than that which was perhaps expected by states which did not enter derogations. The ECtHR referred to the fact that Switzerland had not entered a derogation and, therefore, had been obliged to comply fully with Article 11 within the margin of appreciation afforded to it. Therefore, it appears that states which did not enter derogations may find themselves at a distinct disadvantage in future cases involving measures put in place to respond to the pandemic and would, thus, have been well advised to have entered derogations in respect of such measures. Nevertheless, if Switzerland had derogated, according to Article 15(1), for the measure to have been permissible, it would still have had to have been regarded as being 'strictly required by the exigencies of the situation'. It is at least arguable that if the measure were to pass this test, it would seem that it should also have been regarded as being a proportionate restriction on the right to freedom of assembly under Article 11 on the grounds of protecting health and the rights and freedoms of others.

Under Article 43(1) of the ECHR, 'Within a period of three months from the date of the judgment of the Chamber, any party to the case may, in exceptional cases, request that the case be referred to the Grand Chamber'. On 5 September 2022, *CGAS* was referred to the Grand Chamber at the request of the Swiss government, and a hearing was held on 12 April 2023. As discussed previously, there are significant difficulties with the first instance judgment of the ECtHR in *CGAS*, and it remains to be seen whether these will be remedied by the judgment of the Grand Chamber in this case.

34 As noted earlier, however, under Article 35(1) of the ECHR, the ECtHR may only deal with a matter 'after all domestic remedies have been exhausted, according to the generally recognised rules of international law, and within a period of four months from the date on which the final decision was taken'.

35 App. No. 6865/19, judgment of 11 March 2021.

Pending Applications on Article 11 in the Pandemic Context

There are currently a number of applications pending before the ECtHR which raise similar issues to those considered in *CGAS*. For example, in *Central Unitaria de Traballadores/as v Spain*,[36] the applicant argues that the right to organise and take part in a peaceful demonstration had been breached during the pandemic contrary to Articles 10 and 11. In this case, the applicant is a workers' union which informed the administrative authorities of its intention to hold a demonstration in May 2020. The applicant proposed to apply appropriate sanitary measures to prevent the spread of the COVID-19 virus and expressed its willingness to adopt any other measures which may have been suggested. However, the administrative authorities refused to authorise the demonstration due to the circumstances of the pandemic. On an appeal to the domestic Constitutional Court, the latter weighed up the right to demonstrate and the right to health and, in view of the pandemic context, decided that the latter should prevail.

In *Jarocki v Poland*,[37] the applicant complains that a refusal to authorise a demonstration that he wished to hold in August 2020 violated Article 11. On 21 August 2020 the applicant notified the Mayor of Warsaw that on 29 August 2020, he was planning to hold a two-hour long walking protest against an unlawful police action. The protest was to take place in the street, and the applicant expected that there would be up to 1,000 participants. However, due to the pandemic, a general ban was in force in Poland from 8 August until 10 October 2020 on public assemblies exceeding 150 participants, and on 25 August 2020, the mayor issued a decision forbidding the demonstration. The mayor was of the view that a gathering of 1,000 people would constitute a threat to the health and even to the lives of the participants and the public. The applicant appealed, arguing that the rate of COVID-19 infections was low in the Warsaw region and that the total ban on larger assemblies was, therefore, unjustified and disproportionate. However, the Warsaw Regional Court dismissed the applicant's appeal, as did the Warsaw Court of Appeal. The domestic courts noted that there was a real risk of spreading the COVID-19 virus and that this had to be minimised by, for instance, banning larger public assemblies. The applicant has submitted to the ECtHR detailed calculations of the risk of infection with the COVID-19 virus during a distanced open-air gathering of 1,000 people and argues that the refusal to authorise the demonstration breached his Article 11 right.

36 App. No. 49363/20.
37 App. No. 39750/20.

The pending applications of *Nemytov v Russia*,[38] *Azar v Russia*[39] and *Kostyukhin v Russia*[40] all relate to a prohibition of public events in Moscow which was introduced as a response to the pandemic. In *Nemytov v Russia*, the applicant had staged a solo demonstration in May 2020, during a time when strict lockdown measures were in place. He was arrested and convicted in the administrative proceedings for a breach of rules of conduct during a high alert regime. On 5 June 2020, the applicant then participated in a series of solo demonstrations held by participants in turn, which was subsequently deemed by domestic courts to be a group event in the form of a picket requiring a prior notification. The applicant was sentenced to an administrative fine for a failure to submit a notification of his demonstration. On 25 June 2020, the applicant proceeded to stage a solo demonstration in Red Square in Moscow and was found to be administratively liable for a breach of a ban on public events in the vicinity of the residence of the president of Russia and sentenced to administrative arrest. In *Azar v Russia*, in May 2020, the applicant had also participated in a series of solo demonstrations held by participants in turn, which was subsequently classified by an appellate court as a group event requiring a notification. The applicant was arrested and convicted in administrative proceedings for a repeated breach of rules of conduct of a public event. In *Kostyukhin v Russia*, the applicant had staged a solo demonstration wearing a mask and gloves on 1 August 2020 when the ban on public events still remained in place. He was found administratively liable for a breach of rules of conduct during a high alert regime and sentenced to a fine. The applicants in all three of these cases argue that their rights under Article 11 and also Article 10 of the ECHR were violated. It is interesting to note, however, that although Article 11, the right to freedom of assembly and association, is being invoked in these applications, the demonstrations in which the applicants had engaged were actually solo demonstrations, albeit in certain instances forming part of a series of such demonstrations which were, therefore, deemed to be group events.

However, with its decision in *CGAS*, the ECtHR may already have taken a wrong turn and embarked upon a problematic course from which retreat may be difficult. It is submitted that findings of breaches of the ECHR in instances such as those at issue in these pending applications could be problematic. These applications all concern types of measures which were commonly put in place by many states during the COVID-19 pandemic, and thus, it is arguable that a particularly wide margin of appreciation should be afforded in such cases, given that there is certainly no consensus among states parties that such measures should amount to human rights violations. Indeed, given

38 App. No. 1257/21.
39 App. No. 3244/21.
40 App. No. 24699/21.

the widespread imposition of such measures, the consensus among states would appear to be the precise opposite – that no human rights violations are involved. However, given that the ECtHR has found a breach in *CGAS*, unless this ruling is reversed by the Grand Chamber, it is possible that the Court may be obliged in the interests of consistency to find violations in these cases also, as on their facts, there may be very little to justify a different approach being adopted. Notably, as in *CGAS*, none of the states in question entered derogations in respect of the measures which they adopted in response to the pandemic. If these applications ultimately result in the finding of breaches of the ECHR, numerous further cases could arise, given the very widespread nature of the types of measures in question. This could ultimately lead to the prospect of the ECtHR finding considerable numbers of violations in relation to the measures which were put in place by states to protect lives from a deadly virus at a time when no vaccines were available – measures which were supported by the large majority of the population in the states in question. Such a situation could have the potential to dilute the concept of a human rights violation and damage the legitimacy of human rights law. It is submitted that in its decision in *CGAS*, the ECtHR may have embarked upon a dangerous road from which divergence could prove difficult.

Consideration by the UK Courts of Article 11 and COVID-19 Restrictions

It is noteworthy that, prior to the judgment of the ECtHR in *CGAS*, the compatibility with Article 11 of restrictions on public gatherings in the context of the pandemic had been considered by the domestic courts in the UK. In *R (Dolan) v Secretary of State for Health and Social Care*,[41] (which is discussed further in Chapter 4) the appellants challenged regulations[42] made on 26 March 2020, which they submitted imposed restrictions which were unlawful on various grounds, including that they violated Articles 5, 8, 9 and 11 of the ECHR and Articles 1 and 2 of Protocol No. 1, all of which are guaranteed in domestic law under the Human Rights Act 1998. The appellants sought permission to apply for judicial review of the regulations; however, this was

41 [2020] EWHC 1786 (Admin); [2020] EWCA Civ 1605. For further discussion of this case, see Yap, J. and Jin, N.U., '*R (Dolan) v Secretary of State for Health and Social Care*: Legality in the time of coronavirus' (2021) *Oxford University Undergraduate Law Journal* 171; McGrogan, D., '"It is unarguable that what happened under these regulations amounted to a deprivation of liberty": *Dolan v Secretary of State for Health and Social Care*' (2021) *Public Law* 671; and Sumption, J.P.C., 'COVID-19 and the courts – expediency or law? (2021) 137 *Law Quarterly Review* 353.

42 The Health Protection (Coronavirus, Restrictions) (England) Regulations (SI 2020/350).

refused by Lewis J. in the High Court, who held that there had been no violation of any of the ECHR rights in question. This finding was then upheld by the Court of Appeal.

The Article 11 challenge in this case related to Regulation 7, which in its original form, prohibited gatherings in a public place of more than two people (unless the people were members of the same household or the gathering was for specified purposes such as work). The regulation was later amended to the effect that from 1 June 2020, gatherings of more than six people in a public place, or more than two people indoors, were prohibited, unless the people were from the same household.

Interestingly, in considering the compatibility of these measures with Article 11, the UK courts adopted a position which was diametrically opposed to the approach later taken by the ECtHR in *CGAS.* As in the *CGAS* case, it was accepted in *Dolan* that the measures in question certainly involved a restriction of the right to freedom of assembly and association under Article 11. As Lewis J. stated in the High Court, 'They do restrict the ability of persons to assemble and associate as they may do so only in small groups. They impinge upon the freedom, important in a democratic country, to gather to protest'.[43] As in *CGAS*, the real issue, therefore, related to justification of the restrictions under Article 11(2); however, it was on this point that the UK courts adopted a radically different approach to that of the ECtHR in *CGAS.* According to Lewis J.,

> (The restrictions) pursue a legitimate aim as they are intended to bear down upon the spread of infection by preventing opportunities for the transmission of coronavirus between humans. They are in accordance with law as they were imposed by regulations made pursuant to an Act of Parliament. The issue is whether it is arguable that they are not a proportionate interference … In truth, however, there is no realistic prospect that the courts would find regulation 7 in its current form to be a disproportionate interference with the rights guaranteed by Article 11 of the Convention … The regulation was time-limited and would expire after 6 months in any event. During that period, the government was under a duty to carry out regular reviews and to terminate the restriction if it was no longer necessary to achieve the public health aim of reducing the spread and incidence of coronavirus within the population. In all reality in those circumstances, there is no realistic prospect of a court deciding in these, possibly unique, circumstances that the regulation was a disproportionate interference with the rights guaranteed by Article 11 of the Convention.[44]

43 2020] EWHC 1786 (Admin), at para. 94.
44 At paras. 95–96.

The Court of Appeal, likewise, was of the view that a valid argument could not be made that Article 11 had been violated by the measures in question.

At one level, it is, perhaps, unsurprising that domestic courts may take a more restrictive approach to the scope of Article 11 than that adopted by the ECtHR, which is, of course, the judicial enforcement mechanism of the ECHR itself. Nevertheless, it seems that the approach of the UK courts in *Dolan* has more to commend it than that of the ECtHR in *CGAS*. In his judgment, Lewis J. demonstrated a keen awareness of the circumstances in which the measures in question were adopted, stating that,

> The context in which the regulation was made was one of a pandemic where a highly infectious disease capable of causing death was spreading. The disease was transmissible between humans. The scientific understanding of this novel coronavirus was limited. There was no effective treatment or vaccine. The regulation was intended to restrict the opportunities for transmission between humans. The regulation therefore limits the opportunity for groups of individuals to gather together, whether indoors or outdoors.[45]

Conversely, it appears that such an awareness of the context of the restrictions in *CGAS* was somewhat lacking in the judgment of the ECtHR, as discussed previously.

Notably, Lewis J., in explaining his reasons for his conclusion that the restrictions were not in violation of Article 11, pointed to the fact that the regulation in question was time-limited and would, in any event, expire after six months. Interestingly, the restrictions at issue in *CGAS* could be said to be less stringent and of even more limited temporality. In both cases, the relevant restrictions were implemented in March 2020; however, the restrictions in question in *CGAS* were relaxed in May 2020 to allow for gatherings of up to 30 participants, and the ban on public events was lifted in June 2020, with events involving in excess of 1,000 participants then becoming permissible in August 2020. By contrast, the regulation at issue in *Dolan* was not amended until June 2020, and then only to allow for gatherings of up to six people. Nevertheless, the ECtHR in *CGAS* had pointed to the blanket nature and what the Court viewed as the significant length of the ban on public events as factors leading to the conclusion that the interference with the rights protected by Article 11 had not been proportionate to the aims pursued. However, the restrictions were relaxed after only around two months to allow for gatherings of up to 30 people, which appears to be a short time period, given the competing interests which were at stake, namely the protection of life and public health in the context of a deadly global pandemic. The ban on public events

45 At paras. 95–96.

was then lifted around a month later. By contrast, the regulation in question in *Dolan* was not amended until around three months after its implementation, and then only to allow for gatherings of up to six people. Nevertheless, Lewis J. was adamant that 'there is no realistic prospect that the courts would find regulation 7 in its current form to be a disproportionate interference with the rights guaranteed by Article 11 of the Convention',[46] and, indeed, repeated that 'there is no realistic prospect of a court deciding in these, possibly unique, circumstances that the regulation was a disproportionate interference with the rights guaranteed by Article 11 of the Convention'.[47] Somewhat ironically, around two years after the judgment of Lewis J. was issued, a court, namely the ECtHR, did find that restrictions, which were arguably less stringent than those at issue in *Dolan*, indeed constituted a disproportionate interference with the rights guaranteed by Article 11. If the judgment of the ECtHR in *CGAS* had been issued prior to the decisions of the High Court and Court of Appeal in *Dolan*, it would certainly have been interesting to observe what effect, if any, the ECtHR judgment would have had on the approaches of the domestic courts. Given the definitive position adopted by the domestic courts that there was no chance of the regulation in question being found to be in breach of Article 11, it is a distinct possibility that the domestic courts may well have chosen to disregard the approach taken by the ECtHR in *CGAS*, particularly as this case has been referred to the Grand Chamber, which may adopt a different position to that of the first instance judgment.

Restrictions on Gatherings for Collective Worship

The restrictions on public gatherings which many states imposed in response to the COVID-19 pandemic often involved prohibitions on gatherings for collective worship. Many who would normally have attended gatherings such as church services on a weekly basis (including the author) were supportive of such restrictions, given the risks to life and health posed by the pandemic. Indeed, many churches moved to holding online services and developing a strong online presence through social media, which was of lasting benefit even after the restrictions were lifted.[48] Nevertheless, the inability to gather together for worship was very difficult for many people (including many who, nonetheless, supported the restrictions), and issues surrounding the compatibility of such restrictions with the ECHR have been raised before the ECtHR. Questions relating to the restrictions on gatherings for collective worship adopted in the context of responses of the pandemic and their compliance

46 At para. 95.
47 At para. 96.
48 See for example the Facebook page of the author's own church at https://www.facebook.com/profile.php?id=100066943322103.

with the ECHR do not hinge on the issue of whether they restricted the rights therein – they very clearly restricted the right to freedom of religion under Article 9[49] – but, rather, they centre on the issue of whether these restrictions were legitimate.

The pending application of *Association of Orthodox Ecclesiastical Obedience v Greece*[50] relates to a decision by the Greek authorities to prohibit gatherings for collective worship from 16 March 2020 until 16 May 2020 due to the circumstances arising from the pandemic. On 30 March 2020, the applicant association lodged an application for judicial review of the measures in question. However, on 23 June 2020, the Greek Supreme Administrative Court held that it was unnecessary to rule on the application for judicial review on the basis that the applicant association no longer had a legitimate interest in the matter, as the measure in question had ceased to be applicable. The applicant association argues that its right to freedom of religion under Article 9 and its right of access to a court under Article 6(1) were, thus, violated.

Likewise, in the pending application of *Megard v France*,[51] the applicant argues that a prohibition in the context of the pandemic of any gathering or meeting within religious establishments, with the exception of funeral ceremonies within a limit of 30 people, violated his right under Article 9. Similarly, the pending application of *Figel' v Slovakia*[52] relates to a ban on public religious services. The applicant argues that having been prevented from attending such services breached his rights under Article 9. In particular, he argues that the interference in question was not in accordance with the law, did not pursue a legitimate aim (in that he alleges that there was no scientific evidence for a link between the measure and protection of public health) and was not necessary in a democratic society (in that he alleges that the measure was indiscriminate and that it was not shown that less restrictive measures were insufficient).

As is discussed in Chapter 4, in *Constantin-Lucian Spînu v Romania*,[53] the ECtHR held that measures put in place due to the pandemic which meant that the applicant was no longer permitted to leave prison to attend Adventist Church services did not constitute a violation of his Article 9 right. However, the ECtHR has not yet made a ruling on the compatibility with Article 9 of the

49 Article 9(1) states that, 'Everyone has the right to freedom of thought, conscience and religion; this right includes freedom to change his religion or belief and freedom, either alone or in community with others and in public or private, to manifest his religion or belief, in worship, teaching, practice and observance'. Article 9(2) states that, 'Freedom to manifest one's religion or beliefs shall be subject only to such limitations as are prescribed by law and are necessary in a democratic society in the interests of public safety, for the protection of public order, health or morals, or for the protection of the rights and freedoms of others'.

50 App. No. 52104/20.

51 App. No. 32647/22.

52 App. No. 12131/21.

53 App. No.29443/20, judgment of 11 October 2022.

general prohibitions on gatherings for collective worship which were part of responses to the pandemic in many states.

Nevertheless, it is noteworthy that questions relating to the extent to which the forced closure of places of worship in Scotland due to the pandemic was compatible with Article 9 have been considered by the Court of Session of Scotland in the case of *Philip and Others for Judicial Review of the closure of places of worship in Scotland*.[54] In this case, the 27 petitioners, who were ministers and other church leaders, challenged by judicial review the lawfulness of regulations[55] which forced the closure in January 2021 of places of worship in Scotland as part of the response to the pandemic. It was common ground between the parties that there had been an interference with the petitioners' Article 9 rights and that the issue to be decided was whether the restrictions in question fell within Article 9(2), namely whether they were prescribed by law, pursued a legitimate aim and were necessary in a democratic society in the interests of public health.[56] The court stated that to be prescribed by law, the restrictions 'must both have a basis in domestic law, and be accessible to the persons concerned and be foreseeable as to their effects'.[57] The restrictions in question clearly met these criteria, and it was also accepted by the court that they pursued a legitimate aim within the scope of Article 9(2).

The key issue was, therefore, whether the restrictions were necessary in a democratic society – that is, proportionate. The court stated that assessing this issue involved four stages, namely:

> (i) whether the objective being pursued is sufficiently important to justify the limitation ofa protected right; (ii) whether the measure is rationally connected to the objective; (iii) whether a less intrusive measure could have been used without unacceptably compromising the achievement of the objective; and (iv) whether, balancing the severity of the measure's effect on the rights of the persons to whom it applies against the importance of the objective, to the extent that the measure will contribute to its achievement, the former outweighs the latter.[58]

54 [2021] CSOH 32, paras. 95–127. For further discussion of this case, see Greene, A., 'Closing places of worship and COVID-19: Towards a culture of justification?' (2021) 25 *Edinburgh Law Review* 393.

55 Health Protection (Coronavirus) (Restrictions and Requirements) (Local Levels) (Scotland) Amendment (No 11) Regulations 2021 (SSI 2021/3).

56 Article 9(2) of the ECHR states, 'Freedom to manifest one's religion or beliefs shall be subject only to such limitations as are prescribed by law and are necessary in a democratic society in the interests of public safety, for the protection of public order, health or morals, or for the protection of the rights and freedoms of others'.

57 At para. 98.

58 At para. 100. This test had previously been set out in *Bank Mellat v Her Majesty's Treasury (No 2)* [2013] UKSC 39 at para. 74.

In relation to the first of these stages, it was not in dispute that the aim being pursued – that is, reducing risk in order to protect health and preserve life – was sufficiently important to justify limitation of the right in question. As regards the second stage, the court stated that,

> It is not irrational to conclude that the more people stay at home, the less the virus will be passed on. Accordingly, the Regulations satisfy the rationality stage of the assessment. That said, there is a whiff of irrationality about the decision not even to allow places of worship to open for private prayer, when one looks at the reasoning behind that option not being recommended.[59]

Regarding the third stage, the question was

> whether a less intrusive measure than closing places of worship (on pain of criminal sanctions) could have been used without unacceptably compromising the achievement of the objective of maintaining public health and preserving life by reducing the risk of infection from coronavirus.[60]

On this point, the court was of the view that the respondents had 'failed to show that no less intrusive means than the Regulations were available to address their aim of reducing risk to a significant extent'.[61] As the court stated,

> they have not demonstrated why there was an unacceptable degree of risk by continuing to allow places of worship which employed effective mitigation measures and had good ventilation to admit a limited number of people for communal worship. They have not demonstrated why they could not proceed on the basis that those responsible for places of worship would continue to act responsibly in the manner in which services were conducted, and not open if it was not safe to do so; in other words, why the opening of churches could not have been left to guidance … (T)he respondents have in any event not demonstrated why it was necessary to ban private prayer, the reasons which were given for that recommendation being insufficient to withstand even the lowest degree of scrutiny.[62]

It was, therefore, held that the regulations failed the third stage and, thus, were not a proportionate interference with the rights of the petitioners under Article 9.

59 At para. 103.
60 At para. 104.
61 At para. 115.
62 At para. 116.

The court, nevertheless, also proceeded to consider the fourth stage of the test, which involved weighing up the severity of the effects of the measure against the benefits achieved by the measure. As the court stated,

> A range of factors can be considered at this stage, including, in the present case, the extent to which the measure contributes to the achievement of the aim, in other words, the extent to which the risk is reduced by the Regulations; the importance of the right in issue; the severity of the measure's effects; and whether the decision maker has expertise or information not available to the court.[63]

In relation to the extent to which the measure reduced risk, the court commented that,

> Notwithstanding the greater transmissibility, mitigating factors are known to reduce the risk of transmission, even indoors. Given the relatively low number of instances of persons with Covid-19 known to have attended a place of worship (in comparison with other activities) it is not clear … that the blanket closure of all places of worship can be said to have contributed to a material reduction in risk.[64]

As regards the importance of the right in question, the court stated that, 'it is not clear that the respondents have fully appreciated the importance of article 9 rights',[65] and that 'the right to manifest one's religion is an important right to which much weight must be attached'.[66] In relation to the holding of services online, the court remarked that,

> While some people may derive some benefit from being able to observe on-line services, it is undeniable that certain aspects of certain faiths simply cannot take place, at all, under the current legislative regime: in particular, communion; baptism; and confession, to name but three. It is impossible to measure the effect of those restrictions on those who hold religious beliefs. It goes beyond mere loss of companionship and an inability to attend a lunch club.[67]

The fact that breach of the regulations carried a criminal sanction of a fine of up to £10,000 was also a relevant consideration. The court did consider the

63 At para. 118.
64 At para. 119.
65 At para. 120.
66 At para. 120.
67 At para. 121.

fact that some church leaders agreed with the decision to close churches and considered the regulations to be proportionate, however, decided that such views had to be discounted as 'proportionality is the question the court must decide',[68] and 'it is hardly relevant that some do not object to their rights being interfered with, if others in the same position do'.[69] The court concluded on this point that,

> Ultimately the matter is finely balanced, particularly as … the decision is ultimately a political one and that the respondents do enjoy some margin of appreciation at this stage of the test as at others. Nonetheless, the apparent under-playing of the importance of the article 9 right in comparison with other activities, coupled with the blanket ban on *all* forms of worship, including private prayer, communion, confession and baptism, lead … to the conclusion that even if *some* enforced restriction on the right to worship was justified by the situation in December 2020/January 2021, the Regulations in the form they were passed did have a disproportionate effect and thus that they also fail the fourth stage of the assessment.[70]

The court, thus, held that the regulations constituted a disproportionate interference with the rights of the petitioners under Article 9 and were, therefore, beyond the legislative competence of the respondents.[71]

Philip and Others for Judicial Review of the closure of places of worship in Scotland was, of course, a decision of a domestic court, and the fact that a violation of Article 9 in relation to the closure of places of worship was found in this case does not mean that the same decision would be made by the ECtHR in a similar case. At one level, it could be said to be somewhat peculiar if the ECtHR, the judicial enforcement mechanism of the ECHR, were to take a less expansive view of the scope of the rights contained therein than a domestic court. However, it must be remembered that the factual matrices are not the same in all cases involving the closure of places of worship during the pandemic. As the court itself stated in *Philip*, the decision in this case was not 'that all churches must immediately open or that it is safe for them to do so, or even that no restrictions at all are justified'.[72] Rather, the extent of the ruling was simply that the specific regulations in question 'went further than they were lawfully able to do, in the circumstances which existed when they were made'.[73] The measure at issue in this case related to a closure of places

68 At para. 123.
69 At para. 123.
70 At para. 126.
71 Under Section 6 of the Human Rights Act 1998, it is unlawful for a public authority to act in a way that is incompatible with a right protected by the European Convention on Human Rights.
72 At para. 129.
73 At para. 129.

of worship during a period beginning in January 2021, around 10 months after the start of the pandemic, and indeed, places of worship remained open in England and Wales during this time. Should the measure in question have related to an earlier stage of the pandemic, when arguably there was a greater risk to life and health (and during which places of worship throughout the entirety of the UK were closed), the court may well have reached a different conclusion. Indeed, the petitioners did not question the necessity of closing places of worship during the earlier stages of the pandemic. As McGrogan comments, in *Philip*, the court carried out 'a thorough analysis of the relevant data'.[74] The fact that places of worship were compelled to close in Scotland could be regarded as somewhat anomalous, given that they were open in England and Wales during this time. Also, as the Court of Session pointed out, it appears that insufficient consideration may have been afforded to the question of whether a blanket closure was essential or whether places of worship could have remained open for private prayer. Whether it was necessary for places of worship to close in early 2021 is a question on which views differ. In Northern Ireland, places of worship were required by law to close from March 2020 until July 2020.[75] However, many (including the author's own church) voluntarily decided to remain closed for longer periods of time, for example, until September of that year. The only other time during the pandemic when places of worship were required by law to close in Northern Ireland was for a two-week 'circuit breaker' lockdown which began in late November 2020. Although churches in Northern Ireland were closed again from January 2021 until April 2021, this closure was voluntarily decided upon by an inter-church forum as opposed to being required by law. The general views of the majority of church leaders in Northern Ireland on the question of whether it was necessary for places of worship to close during the early part of 2021 was, therefore, contrary to that of the views of the petitioners in *Philip* as to the necessity for such closures in Scotland.

The approach which the ECtHR will take in a case involving an Article 9 challenge to measures involving the closure of places of worship during the pandemic, therefore, remains to be seen. It is notable that in the pending application of *Association of Orthodox Ecclesiastical Obedience v Greece*,[76] the prohibition of gatherings for collective worship at issue in this case applied at the beginning of the pandemic, from 16 March 2020 until 16 May 2020, when the risk to life and to public health was arguably at its height. If the ECtHR were to hold that such a prohibition was a disproportionate interference with Article 9, such a finding would thus go beyond the decision of the

74 McGrogan, op. cit., at p. 677.

75 Regulation 4(5) of the Health Protection (Coronavirus, Restrictions) Regulations (Northern Ireland) 2020.

76 App. No. 52104/20.

Court of Session in *Philip*, in which the finding of a breach of Article 9 related to measures imposed during a later stage in the pandemic when arguably a lower risk pertained. Nevertheless, given that the ECtHR found a breach of Article 11 in the *CGAS* case in relation to restrictions imposed at the start of the pandemic on public gatherings more generally, it is possible that the Court may find a violation of Article 9 in *Association of Orthodox Ecclesiastical Obedience*, particularly as, similar to *CGAS*, questions have been raised in this case concerning the availability of judicial review in the domestic courts of the measure in question. The measures at issue in *Megard v France*[77] and *Figel' v Slovakia*[78] relate to later stages of the pandemic when arguably a lesser degree of risk pertained; however, it is possible that the ECtHR could adopt a similar approach to that of the Court of Session in *Philip* in these cases.

Conclusion

In conclusion, as was discussed in this chapter, generally one of the most prominent aspects of the responses of states to the pandemic was to put in place measures prohibiting or restricting public gatherings, thus raising issues regarding, in particular, the right to freedom of assembly and association under Article 11 of the ECHR, as was demonstrated in the *CGAS* case. However, as was asserted in this chapter, the Court's finding of a violation in this case was arguably problematic. At a time when the discourse of human rights is currently coming under sustained questioning, it is argued that the ECtHR should be cautious of finding breaches of the ECHR in cases involving public restrictions which were applied for the purpose of protecting life and health in response to a global pandemic. It has been established by the Court that when there is no consensus among states parties, a wider margin of appreciation should be afforded. There was certainly no consensus among states parties against the type of measure in question in *CGAS* – any consensus was actually in favour of this type of measure given that it appears to have been very much in line with those imposed by many other states in Europe and beyond. Indeed, it is submitted that cases such as *CGAS* constitute paradigm examples of an area in which a wide margin of appreciation should be granted to states. To do otherwise leaves the ECtHR open to criticism regarding 'the overreach of human rights law'.[79]

77 App. No. 32647/22.

78 App. No. 12131/21.

79 De Búrca, *Reframing Human Rights in a Turbulent Era*, 2021, Oxford University Press, Oxford, at 4. See further Hannum, H., *Rescuing Human Rights: A Radically Moderate Approach*, 2019, Cambridge University Press, Cambridge.

The *CGAS* case has, however, been referred to the Grand Chamber, and it remains to be seen whether the difficulties with the first instance judgment of the ECtHR in this case will be remedied by the judgment of the Grand Chamber. As was also discussed, there are currently a number of applications pending before the ECtHR which raise similar issues to those considered in *CGAS*. However, with its decision in this case, the ECtHR may already have taken a wrong turn and embarked upon a problematic course from which retreat may be difficult unless the Grand Chamber ultimately reverses the first instance ruling. In addition, the chapter noted that prior to the judgment of the ECtHR in *CGAS*, the compatibility with Article 11 of restrictions on public gatherings in the context of the pandemic had been considered by the domestic courts in the UK in *Dolan*. In this case, in considering the compatibility with Article 11 of arguably more stringent measures than those at issue in *CGAS*, the UK courts adopted a position which was diametrically opposed to the approach later taken by the ECtHR in the *CGAS* case. As argued in this chapter, the approach of the UK courts in *Dolan* appears to have more to commend it than that of the ECtHR in *CGAS*.

The measures adopted by states in response to the COVID-19 pandemic were not, of course, limited to restrictions on public gatherings; rather, they impacted upon the lives of individuals in a wide range of other ways which also engaged various provisions of the ECHR and in relation to which issues have been raised before the ECtHR, as will be discussed in Chapter 4.

4 The ECHR and Other COVID-19 Restrictions

The measures adopted by states in response to the COVID-19 pandemic were not, of course, limited to restrictions on public gatherings. Rather, they impacted upon the lives of individuals in a wide range of other ways which also engaged various provisions of the ECHR and in relation to which issues have been raised before the ECtHR, as is discussed in this chapter. For example, during April 2020, almost half of the world's population were in lockdown,[1] which meant that people could leave their homes only for a very limited range of reasons. Another common feature of the measures adopted by states due to the pandemic involved schools being required to teach pupils, partly or wholly, through online methods as opposed to in-person classes. As lockdown measures eased, many states then imposed a 'health pass' system as an interim stage between lockdown and full easing of restrictions. Requirements to wear face coverings when in indoor public settings such as shops were also a common response. Another type of measure which was adopted in a number of states was a requirement for those employed in certain sectors to be vaccinated against COVID-19, and there were also other measures implemented due to the pandemic which impacted upon employment and professional activity. For example, the adoption of measures which required many shops and other businesses to close for certain periods of time was a common response by states. In addition, whilst states had particular duties under Article 2 (the right to life) and 3 (the right to be free from torture or inhuman or degrading treatment) to adopt protective measures against COVID-19 in respect of prisoners and detainees, as was considered in Chapter 2, it is also the case that measures implemented to prevent the spread of the virus raised particular human rights issues for such persons and, in some instances, had an impact upon criminal proceedings. In certain cases, measures adopted in the context of the pandemic also raised particular issues for asylum seekers. This chapter explores questions which have been raised before the ECtHR in respect of these issues.

1 Euronews, 'Coronavirus: Half of humanity now on lockdown as 90 countries call for confinement', 3 April 2020, https://www.euronews.com/2020/04/02/coronavirus-in-europe-spain-s-death-toll-hits-10-000-after-record-950-new-deaths-in-24-hou

DOI: 10.4324/9781003383437-4

Lockdown Measures

As was discussed in Chapter 3, one of the most prominent aspects of the responses of states to the pandemic was to put in place measures prohibiting or restricting public gatherings. An equally prevalent feature of such responses was to impose unprecedented lockdown measures which only permitted individuals to leave their homes for a strictly limited range of reasons.[2] For example, UK government guidance stated that people should leave home only to shop for basic necessities such as food and medicine, one form of exercise per day, medical need or to provide care or help to a vulnerable person and travelling to and from work, but only when work could not be done from home. Even when the activity in question fell within one of these four categories, the amount of time spent away from home had to be minimised as far as possible.[3] Lockdown measures were indisputably an essential response to the pandemic. As was discussed in Chapter 1, COVID-19 was a deadly new virus about which little was known during the early stages of the pandemic and for which there was no vaccine. In such circumstances, measures which strictly limited contact were the only option open to states to adopt and were undoubtedly essential to protect the rights of citizens under Articles 2 and 3 of the ECHR, as was discussed in Chapter 2.

Nevertheless, it is not disputed that lockdown measures certainly constituted restrictions on rights contained in the ECHR. As with the restrictions on public gatherings which were discussed in Chapter 3, issues surrounding lockdown measures adopted by states parties due to the pandemic and their compliance with the ECHR do not hinge on the question of whether they restricted the rights therein – they undoubtedly did – but, rather, they relate to the issue of whether these restrictions were legitimate. Such questions have now been raised before the ECtHR.

Terhes v Romania[4] was an admissibility decision of 20 May 2021 which concerned the lockdown measure which had been imposed by Romania from 24 March 2020 until 14 May 2020. Under this measure, no movement outside the home was permissible, apart from a certain number of circumstances and on production of a document attesting to valid reasons for leaving the home. Individuals who breached the regulations were liable to a fine. The applicant argued that this measure violated his right to liberty under Article 5 of the ECHR. However, the measure in question had been imposed under a state

2 See for example, the Health Protection (Coronavirus, Restrictions) (England) Regulations 2020 (SI 2020/350).

3 BBC News, 'Coronavirus: Strict new curbs on life in UK announced by PM', 24 March 2020, https://www.bbc.co.uk/news/uk-52012432. See Cabinet Office, 'Guidance: Staying at home and away from others (social distancing)', updated 1 May 2020, https://www.gov.uk/government/publications/full-guidance-on-staying-at-home-and-away-from-others/full-guidance-on-staying-at-home-and-away-from-others.

4 App. No. 49933/20, decision of 20 May 2021.

of emergency with the aim of confining the entire population due to a public health situation which the authorities viewed as being urgent and serious. Under Romanian law, in the event of a state of emergency, a set of exceptional measures could be adopted which derogated from the established constitutional order. A state of emergency could be declared in the event of actual or imminent danger, for a specified period of time, and this allowed the state to take measures restricting the exercise of particular fundamental freedoms. The president of Romania had declared the state of emergency after consulting with the competent bodies and on account of the exceptional and unforeseeable circumstances created by COVID-19 pandemic. The introduction of emergency measures, including lockdown, had been aimed at mitigating the social and economic impact of the pandemic and safeguarding the right to life. The ECtHR was of the view that the COVID-19 pandemic did indeed constitute exceptional and unforeseeable circumstances, as it was liable to have very serious consequences for health, society, the economy and the functioning of the state and life in general.

The lockdown measure had been imposed for 52 days and had been a general measure imposed on the whole population. The applicant had been required to remain at home, being permitted to leave only for one of the reasons stipulated in the relevant legislation and with the necessary exemption form. However, the ECtHR pointed out that he had been free to leave his home for a range of reasons and could go to various places at whatever time the situation required. He had not been subject to individual surveillance and did not claim to have been forced to live in a cramped space, nor had he been deprived of all social contact. The Court was, therefore, of the view that the measure in question could not be equated with house arrest. In addition, the applicant had not explained in concrete terms how the measure had affected him. He did not allege that he had been confined indoors for the whole duration of the state of emergency, and he had not provided any specific information regarding his own particular experience of lockdown.

The ECtHR, thus, concluded that the level of intensity of the restrictions on the applicant's freedom of movement had not been such that the lockdown could constitute a deprivation of liberty. There had, therefore, been no violation of the right to liberty under Article 5, and the Court declared the application to be inadmissible as being incompatible with the provisions of the ECHR. The ECtHR noted that Romania had announced its intention to derogate from the right to freedom of movement under Article 2 of Protocol No. 4. However, the applicant had not asserted this right and, given that Article 5 was not applicable, it was not necessary to examine the validity of the derogation.

Although *Terhes* was an admissibility decision, as opposed to a full judgment on the merits of the case, the decision, nevertheless, served to establish that the lockdown measures which had been put in place by many states, of which the Romanian measure was typical, were not in breach of Article 5.

However, as the applicant had not relied upon the right to freedom of movement under Article 2 of Protocol No. 4, the decision still left open the question of whether lockdown measures may be in breach of this provision.

However, on 5 July 2022 another admissibility decision regarding measures which had been taken in Romania regarding the COVID-19 pandemic was issued by the ECtHR. *Piperea v Romania*[5] related to a later phase in the state's response to the pandemic. In this case, the applicant argued that a declaration of a state of alert which had been issued in Romania on 18 May 2020, and then extended repeatedly until 8 March 2022, had violated his rights to respect for private and family life under Article 8 and to freedom of movement under Article 2 of Protocol No. 4, as it imposed a requirement for individuals leaving home in certain circumstances to complete a document stating where they were going, why and for how long and providing other personal information. In addition, the applicant, who was a university professor, objected to social distancing and complained that distancing from students interfered with his ability to perform his teaching duties effectively. He also took issue with the requirement to wear a mask and the need to isolate for a particular number of days in the event of a positive test for COVID-19, measures which he believed were unnecessary and inadequate.

The ECtHR pointed out that the measures in question had been introduced as part of the state of alert declared in Romania for public health reasons, following the state of emergency which had been declared in March 2020. The measures had been imposed on the entire population in response to what the national authorities had deemed to be a serious public health situation. The applicant had not provided information about his individual situation or explained in specific terms how the national authorities' alleged failures affected him directly. Article 34 of the ECHR states that, 'The Court may receive applications from any person, nongovernmental organisation or group of individuals claiming to be the victim of a violation by one of the High Contracting Parties of the rights set forth in the Convention or the Protocols thereto'. Under Article 35(3), the ECtHR shall declare inadmissible any individual application if it considers that:

(a) The application is incompatible with the provisions of the Convention or the Protocols thereto, manifestly ill-founded, or an abuse of the right of individual application; or
(b) The applicant has not suffered a significant disadvantage, unless respect for human rights as defined in the Convention and the Protocols thereto requires an examination of the application on the merits.

5 App. No. 24183/21, decision of 5 July 2022.

The ECtHR noted that Article 34 does not allow for breaches of the ECHR to be complained of in the abstract and does not afford applicants a right of action exercisable purely in the public interest. Applicants must substantiate their complaints by putting before the Court specific facts and evidence and by explaining why they are of the view that the provision on which they are relying has been violated. However, the ECtHR stated that the applicant had simply alleged a restriction on his right to freedom of movement under Article 2 of Protocol No. 4 without further substantiating his complaint. In relation to the alleged breach of the applicant's right to respect for his private life under Article 8 of the ECHR, the Court noted that he had not specified whether he had actually been asked to show his papers when going anywhere nor in what concrete way his right to respect for his private life had been impaired. The applicant had not explained in specific terms how the measures had affected him nor had he put forward any precise information regarding his actual experience of that period. The ECtHR was, therefore, of the view that the application either did not meet the admissibility criteria set out in Articles 34 and 35 or did not disclose any appearance of a breach of the rights contained in the ECHR and the protocols thereto.

On the same date as that of the decision of the ECtHR in *Piperea*, the Court also issued an admissibility decision in another application involving a complaint regarding lockdown measures which had been imposed, in this instance by Croatia. In *Magdic v Croatia*[6] (which was also discussed in Chapter 3), the applicant complained about measures which had been in place from 19 March 2020 until 11 May 2020 in order to contain the spread of the COVID-19 virus which prohibited all public events and gatherings of more than five persons in one place and suspended the work of all shops except those which were essential, such as pharmacies and grocery stores. Religious gatherings were also suspended. From 23 March 2020, a further measure had been put in place whereby people were not permitted to leave their territorial unit (that is, their county) except for justified reasons such as travelling for work which could not be done from home or taking care of a family member. The applicant argued that these measures had breached his right to freedom of assembly under Article 11 of the ECHR, his right to freedom of religion under Article 9, and his right to freedom of movement under Article 2 of Protocol No. 4. In response, the ECtHR pointed out that should an applicant wish to complain of a violation of their rights, in order to demonstrate the victim status necessary under Article 34 to bring a case, 'they must produce reasonable and convincing evidence of the likelihood that a violation affecting them personally will occur; mere suspicion or conjecture is insufficient in this respect'.[7] However, in deeming the application to be inadmissible, the ECtHR

6 App. No. 17578/20, decision of 5 July 2022.

7 At para. 9.

stated that the applicant had not provided any information regarding his personal situation beyond his identity and his occupation. He had provided no information to demonstrate how precisely the measures in question affected or would be likely to affect him directly or target him due to any possible individual characteristics. For example, although the applicant alleged that his right to freedom of movement had been violated, he had not mentioned where and when he had intended to travel and had been prevented from doing so due to the measures in question. Likewise, whilst the applicant complained that the measures had breached his right to freedom of religion, he had not indicated to which religious community he belonged. The ECtHR could not, therefore, conduct an individual assessment of the applicant's situation and stated that, 'It thus appears that the applicant wishes to complain about the impugned measures in a general manner, contemplating that, as a result of their adoption, his freedoms were automatically violated'.[8] As in *Piperea*, the Court was of the view that the applicant could not be regarded as a victim for the purposes of Article 34 of the ECHR, and, therefore, the application was incompatible with the provisions of the Convention within the meaning of Article 35(3)(a) and must be rejected.

Both *Piperea* and *Magdic* serve to emphasise the point that was made in Chapters 2 and 3 – if seeking to bring a complaint before the ECtHR regarding state responses to the COVID-19 pandemic, an applicant must be very careful to explain how any alleged violations of the ECHR affected them at an individual level. Under Article 34, in order to have standing to take a case, an individual must show that they were 'directly affected' by the measure in question. In the context of restrictions implemented by states in the circumstances of the pandemic, it is not, therefore, sufficient simply to allege a violation of an ECHR right due to a general measure affecting the entire population which has been put in place. Rather an applicant must present the ECtHR with specific facts and evidence, explain why they are of the view that the provision on which they are relying has been breached and specify in precise terms how the measure in question actually affected them personally.

In addition, it is noteworthy that the compatibility of the lockdown regulations imposed in England in response to the pandemic with various provisions of the ECHR has been examined by the domestic courts in the UK. As was referred to in Chapter 3, in *R (Dolan) v Secretary of State for Health and Social Care*,[9] the appellants challenged regulations[10] made on 26 March 2020 which they submitted imposed restrictions that were unlawful on various grounds, including that they violated Articles 5, 8, 9 and 11 of the ECHR and Articles 1 and 2 of Protocol No. 1, all of which are guaranteed in domestic

8 At para. 11.
9 [2020] EWHC 1786 (Admin); [2020] EWCA Civ 1605.
10 The Health Protection (Coronavirus, Restrictions) (England) Regulations (SI 2020/350).

law under the Human Rights Act 1998. Under the regulations in their original form, certain businesses had to close, places of worship had to close apart from limited purposes such as funerals, people were prohibited from leaving their homes unless they had a reasonable excuse for doing so and gatherings of more than two people in a public place were prohibited unless those involved were members the same household or were gathering for specified purposes such as work.

The first appellant was a British citizen who lived in Monaco. He was the owner of businesses based in the UK and visited the UK to see family and friends. In his evidence, he stated that, if it had been permitted under the regulations, he would have wanted to join in protests against these regulations. The second appellant was a British citizen who worked for a company owned by the first appellant. From late March until June 2020, her 10-year-old son did not attend school, and from 2 June 2020, he attended school for only two days a week. Neither the second appellant nor her son were able to attend mass at church during the relevant time. The third appellant was a pupil at school. The appellants sought permission to apply for judicial review of the regulations; however, this was refused by Lewis J. in the High Court. Lewis J. held that there had been no violation of any ECHR rights, a finding which was upheld by the Court of Appeal.

As in the decision of the ECtHR in *Terhes*, the Court of Appeal in *Dolan* likewise held that the lockdown measures had not involved a deprivation of liberty within the meaning of Article 5. According to the Court of Appeal, it was 'a mischaracterisation to refer to what happened under the regulations as amounting in effect to house arrest or even a curfew'.[11] Rather, 'The obligation to stay at home … was subject to numerous, express exceptions, which were non-exhaustive, and the overriding exception of having a reasonable excuse'.[12]

In relation to Article 8, the Court of Appeal stated that,

> There can be no doubt that the regulations did constitute an interference with article 8 but it is clear that such interference was justified under article 8(2).[13] It was clearly in accordance with law. It pursued a legitimate aim: the protection of health. The interference was unarguably proportionate.[14]

11 [2020] EWCA Civ 1605, at para. 93.
12 At para. 93.
13 Article 8(2) of the ECHR states, 'There shall be no interference by a public authority with the exercise of this right except such as is in accordance with the law and is necessary in a democratic society in the interests of national security, public safety or the economic well-being of the country, for the prevention of disorder or crime, for the protection of health or morals, or for the protection of the rights and freedoms of others'.
14 At para. 96.

In the High Court, Lewis J. had likewise stated that,

> Any interference is proportionate. The restrictions are limited. Persons remain free to live with family members or friends forming part of their household. They may communicate with other and family members by means of communication such as telephones and, if available, internet facilities. They may physically meet family and friends outdoors (subject to the restrictions on numbers …). Given the limited nature of the restrictions, the gravity of the threat posed by the transmission of coronavirus, the fact that the Regulations last for a limited period and have to be reviewed regularly during that period, and restrictions must be terminated as soon as no longer necessary to meet the public health threat, there is no prospect of the current regulations, at the current time, being found to be a disproportionate interference with the rights conferred by Article 8 of the Convention. The contrary is not, in truth, arguable.[15]

Likewise, the Court of Appeal commented that,

> In this context, as in the case of the other qualified rights, we consider that a wide margin of judgement must be afforded to the Government and to Parliament. This is on the well-established grounds both of democratic accountability and institutional competence. We bear in mind that the Secretary of State had access to expert advice which was particularly important in the context of a new virus and where scientific knowledge was inevitably developing at a fast pace. The fact that others may disagree with some of those expert views is neither here nor there. The Government was entitled to proceed on the basis of the advice which it was receiving and balance the public health advice with other matters.[16]

As was discussed in Chapter 3, in relation to questions surrounding the application of Article 11, the right to freedom of assembly and association, to prohibitions on restrictions on public gatherings, the UK domestic courts in *Dolan* took an approach which seemed to be diametrically opposed to that which was later adopted by the ECtHR in *Communauté Genevoise D'Action Syndicale (CGAS) v Switzerland.*[17] However, regarding the compatibility of lockdown restrictions with Article 5, both the domestic courts and the ECtHR are in agreement – such restrictions did not violate this provision. The UK has not ratified Protocol No. 4, and, therefore, the right to freedom of movement has not been incorporated into UK law by the Human Rights Act 1998 and

15 [2020] EWHC 1786 (Admin) at para. 78.
16 [2020] EWCA Civ 1605 at para. 97.
17 App. No. 21881/20, judgment of 15 March 2022.

could not be relied upon by the appellants in *Dolan*. Nevertheless, in addition to relying on Article 5, the appellants did argue that the lockdown measures violated Article 8, an argument which was roundly rejected in both the High Court and Court of Appeal decisions on the basis that any interference with this right was lawful and proportionate to the legitimate aims sought to be achieved. As noted previously, the ECtHR has not yet made a substantive ruling on the compatibility of such lockdown measures with Article 8, or indeed with Article 2 of Protocol No. 4, due to the failure of the applicants in both *Piperea* and *Magdic* to explain how the alleged violations in question affected them at an individual level. It remains to be seen how the ECtHR would approach a case raising such issues in which an applicant has demonstrated the necessary standing to do so.

Restrictions on Schools

Another common feature of the measures adopted by states due to the pandemic involved restrictions being placed on schools. In the pending application of *M.C.K. and M.H.K.-B. and Others v Germany*,[18] the applicants are pupils from various districts in Germany who attended schools which had been subject to restrictions during the COVID-19 pandemic. The German Protection Against Infection Act prescribed for schools, depending on the rate of new COVID-19 infections, a hybrid learning requirement, with school classes divided into different groups alternating between in-person lessons at school and remote learning from home or a complete ban on in-person lessons. The applicants argue that this measure violated their right to respect for private and family life under Article 8 of the ECHR and their right to education under Article 2 of Protocol No. 1 on the basis that these restrictions adversely affected their personal and social development and their mental health as well as reduced the level of their learning and knowledge, which would affect their future careers and income.

Similar issues to those being raised in *M.C.K. and M.H.K.-B. and Others* have been considered by the Court of Appeal of England and Wales in *Dolan*. In this case, as discussed earlier in the chapter, due to restrictions put in place in response to the pandemic from late March until June 2020, the second appellant's 10-year-old son did not attend school, and from 2 June 2020, he attended school for only two days a week. The third appellant was also a pupil at school. The appellants argued that the restrictions in questions violated the right to education under Article 2 of Protocol No. 1. However, according to the Court of Appeal,

18 App. No. 26657/22.

> The fundamental problem for the appellants' submission is that there was no order by the Education Secretary or Government that schools had to close. Nor was there any order that all education had to cease. The wish of all concerned, including the Education Secretary, was that schoolchildren should receive education by remote means, for example through online instruction.[19]

The Court of Appeal then proceeded to state that,

> Further and in any event, article 2 of the First Protocol, reflecting a theme which runs throughout the Convention, envisages a fair balance having to be struck between the rights of the individual and the general interests of the community. In the exceptional circumstances of the pandemic, there is no arguable ground on which a court could interfere with the actions of the Government in this respect.[20]

Notably, the Court of Appeal in *Dolan* seemed to be of the view that the measures in question, although placing restrictions on schools, did not actually restrict the right to education and that this right would only have been restricted if schools had to close in the sense that all education had to cease. It appears that the Court of Appeal was of the opinion that the fact that education continued through online methods meant that the right to education was not restricted, even though pupils were not physically present in schools. It is debatable whether the ECtHR would adopt such a position in *M.C.K. and M.H.K.-B. and Others*. It is true that Article 2 of Protocol No. 1 states simply that, 'No person shall be denied the right to education', and then proceeds to specify only that, 'In the exercise of any functions which it assumes in relation to education and to teaching, the State shall respect the right of parents to ensure such education and teaching in conformity with their own religious and philosophical convictions'. There is certainly no mention of a requirement that education must be carried out through pupils being physically present in school buildings. Indeed, according to the 'Guide on Article 2 of Protocol No. 1 to the European Convention on Human Rights' produced by the Registry of the ECtHR, this provision is

> distinguished by its negative wording which means that the Contracting Parties do not recognise such a right to education as would require them to establish at their own expense, or to subsidise, education of any particular type or at any particular level.[21]

19 [2020] EWCA Civ 1605, at para. 112.
20 At para. 113.
21 Registry of the European Court of Human Rights, 'Guide on Article 2 of Protocol No. 1 to the European Convention on Human Rights', updated on 31 August 2022, https://www.echr.coe.int/documents/guide_art_2_protocol_1_eng.pdf, at para. 3.

The view of the Court of Appeal in *Dolan* does, therefore, seem to have much to commend it.

Nevertheless, even if a more expansive approach to the right to education were to be taken by the ECtHR in *M.C.K. and M.H.K.-B. and Others*, it is very likely that the Court would be of the opinion that the measures in question constituted proportionate restrictions on this right. Interestingly, a literal reading of Article 2 of Protocol No. 1 could lead to the conclusion that the right to education is absolute, given that the provision is phrased simply as, 'No person shall be denied the right to education' with no further qualification. However, according to the Registry of the ECtHR,

> The right to education is not absolute ... as it may give rise to implicitly accepted limitations ... Consequently, the domestic authorities enjoy in such matters a certain margin of appreciation, although the final decision as to the observance of the Convention's requirements rests with the Court. In order to ensure that the restrictions that are imposed do not curtail the right in question to such an extent as to impair its very essence and deprive it of its effectiveness, the Court must satisfy itself that they are foreseeable for those concerned and pursue a legitimate aim.[22]

Indeed, it seems that the range of legitimate aims pursuant to which restrictions on the right to education may be imposed is actually wider than those which pertain, for example, to Articles 8–11 of the ECHR. According to the Registry of the ECtHR,

> Unlike the position with respect to Articles 8 to 11 of the Convention, the permitted restrictions are not bound by an exhaustive list of 'legitimate aims' under Article 2 of Protocol No. 1. Furthermore, a limitation of the right to education will only be compatible with Article 2 of Protocol No. 1 if there is a reasonable relationship of proportionality between the means employed and the aim sought to be achieved.[23]

Given that school settings normally involve large numbers of pupils in very close contact, it would seem that a move to online learning in the context of the pandemic constituted a proportionate measure with the legitimate aims of protecting life and health. The Court of Appeal in *Dolan* was certainly very strongly of this view, stating, as noted previously, that, 'In the exceptional circumstances of the pandemic, there is no arguable ground on which a court could interfere with the actions of the Government in this respect'.[24]

22 Registry of the European Court of Human Rights, op. cit., at para. 5.
23 Registry of the European Court of Human Rights, op. cit., at para. 6.
24 At para. 113.

Health Passes

As lockdown measures eased, many states imposed a 'health pass' system as an interim stage between lockdown and full easing of the COVID-19 restrictions. Under such systems, individuals were typically required to show proof of vaccination against COVID-19, proof of having recently recovered from COVID-19 or evidence of having tested negative for the virus in order to enter certain premises such as restaurants and other hospitality venues. The compatibility of such measures with the provisions of the ECHR was the subject of the admissibility decision in *Zambrano v France*.[25] Interestingly, the difficult issues faced by states when responding to the COVID-19 pandemic is demonstrated by the fact that in *Le Mailloux v France*,[26] which was discussed in Chapter 2, the applicant essentially argued that France had not done enough to protect individuals from COVID-19, whilst in *Zambrano v France*, the applicant alleged that measures taken by France had been excessive.

In *Zambrano*, the applicant's complaint related to a 'health pass' which had been introduced in France. Such a pass was required, for example, in order to enter restaurants and bars or to use long-distance public transport by train, coach or aeroplane. The health pass was mandatory for adults wishing to take part in activities in the relevant premises and for staff working in them. Penalties could be imposed on the public for failure to present a health pass or for fraudulent use of such a pass and on the business owners and staff responsible for checking health passes should they fail to comply with the requirement to do so. The applicant relied on Articles 3 and 8 of the ECHR as well as on Article 14 of the ECHR and Article 1 of Protocol No. 12, both of which relate to non-discrimination, although the ECtHR noted in its decision that Protocol No. 12 had not actually been ratified by France. The applicant argued that the health pass system constituted a discriminatory interference with the right to respect for private life and was intended to compel individuals to get vaccinated. Somewhat unusually, he had suggested on his website that members of the public complete a particular pre-filled form in order to increase the number of applications to the ECtHR in an effort to cause congestion and to paralyse the operations of the Court.

The ECtHR declared the application to be inadmissible due to a failure to exhaust domestic remedies[27] and to the fact that the application constituted an

25 App. No. 41994/21, decision of 7 October 2021.

26 App. No. 18108/20, decision of 5 November 2020.

27 Article 35(1) of the ECHR provides that, 'The Court may only deal with the matter after all domestic remedies have been exhausted'.

abuse of the right of individual petition.[28] The Court also commented that the applicant had not demonstrated that he had been subjected to any coercion as a person who did not wish to be vaccinated. The laws in question did not impose any general obligation to be vaccinated, nor did they impose vaccination on persons wishing to undertake certain journeys or to access certain premises. On the contrary, a choice of documents could be presented – the result of a negative COVID-19 test, proof of full vaccination against COVID-19, or a certificate showing recovery from the virus.

Although *Zambrano* was an admissibility decision, as opposed to a full judgment of the ECtHR, the case, nevertheless, indicates that 'health pass' systems will not be deemed to constitute a violation of the provisions of the ECHR. Given that the aims of such systems were to protect the lives and health of individuals from the COVID-19 virus, it seems that this is the correct approach.

Notably, the health pass system imposed in Northern Ireland in response to the pandemic and its compatibility with provisions of the ECHR has been examined by the domestic courts. *In the Matter of an Application by Risteard O'Murchu for Leave to Apply for Judicial Review v The Department of Health for Northern Ireland*[29] involved an applicant who sought leave to apply for judicial review of a system which came into operation in Northern Ireland on 29 November 2021,[30] under which COVID-status certification was required to enter various settings such as licensed hospitality premises which served food and/or drink on the premises, cinemas, theatres, conference halls and nightclubs. Such settings could admit only 'qualifying persons' who could evidence proof of full vaccination against COVID-19, a negative COVID-19 test taken within the previous 48 hours, proof of recovery from COVID-19 following a positive test within the previous 30–180 days, confirmation in writing of participation in a clinical trial for vaccination against COVID-19 or evidence of medical exemption. The applicant, who had not been vaccinated, argued that this system violated his rights under Articles 8 and 14 of the ECHR.

The High Court accepted that the restrictions in question arguably engaged the applicant's rights under Article 8, given that they imposed a restriction on his ability to attend certain social venues and that if he did attend such venues, he was required to disclose aspects of his medical status. It was, therefore, for the proposed respondent to justify such an interference by establishing that there was a legal basis for the interference, that the policy behind the interference pursued a legitimate aim, that the interference

28 Under Article 35(3)(a) of the ECHR, the Court shall declare inadmissible any individual application if it considers that the application is manifestly ill-founded.

29 [2022] NIQB 13; [2023] NICA 28.

30 The Health Protection (Coronavirus, Restrictions) Regulations (Northern Ireland) 2021 (Amendment No: 19) Regulations (Northern Ireland) 2021.

was necessary in a democratic society and that the interference was proportionate. The Court was of the view that there was clearly a basis in law for the establishment of the system and that the scheme pursued the legitimate policy aims of protecting the health of the population by limiting the spread of the COVID-19 virus, seeking to ensure that the health care system had the capacity to care for patients and allowing higher risk settings to continue to operate.

In relation to whether the interference was 'necessary in a democratic society', the High Court stated that,

> In accordance with well-established jurisprudence 'necessary' needs to be construed as 'reasonably necessary' rather than absolutely or strictly necessary. To a large extent this issue turns on the applicant's central submission that there is no, or insufficient, scientific justification for the introduction of the measures. In the court's view this submission is misconceived … What … is unarguable is the fact that vaccination reduces the risk of becoming infected with the virus. Thus, those who attend 'high risk settings' and who are vaccinated are less likely to be infected and inevitably therefore there is less risk of vaccinated persons, or those with a negative test, transmitting the infection.[31]

The Court proceeded to state that in assessing whether the interference was necessary or proportionate, it took into account a number of matters, including the fact that those who attended venues subject to the scheme could do so in the knowledge that they were mixing with persons who were less likely to be infected with the virus, there was scientific evidence to support the argument that restricting access to vaccinated or non-infected persons in high risk settings had the potential to reduce the spread of the COVID-19 virus, the scheme had been implemented in the context of a deteriorating situation in local hospitals and had the support of the Chief Medical Officer and the Chief Scientific Advisor, an alternative method of certification had been provided for those who had not been vaccinated and the scheme had been kept under review.

The High Court was, thus, of the view that,

> Although the court accepts that arguably there has been interference with the applicant's Article 8 rights it considers that this interference was limited. He was not prohibited from attending high risk settings identified in the scheme. It was open to him to avail of the option of proof of a negative lateral flow test within the previous 48 hours. It is noted that such tests are

31 [2022] NIQB 13, at para. 39.

> free and easily available in this jurisdiction … That inconvenience has to be seen in light of the legitimate and overwhelming aim of protecting public health.[32]

In relation to the applicant's argument that the health pass scheme was in breach of Article 14 in conjunction with Article 8, the Court opined that the applicant had put forward no evidential basis for such a claim.

The High Court commented that, 'There is ample authority that the state enjoys a wide margin of appreciation in making the judgement calls on issues of this type',[33] and concluded that 'the regulations at issue were in accordance with the law and served a legitimate aim and were proportionate and justifiable'.[34] In the Court's view, the case was 'unarguable' and had 'no realistic prospect of success'.[35] Leave to apply for judicial review was, therefore, rejected, a decision which was later upheld by the Court of Appeal.[36]

Requirements to Wear Masks

During the COVID-19 pandemic, many states imposed requirements to wear face coverings when in indoor public settings such as shops as a way of limiting the spread of the virus. As the World Health Organization stated, 'Masks are a key measure to reduce transmission and save lives … Depending on the type, masks can be used for either protection of healthy persons or to prevent onward transmission, or both'.[37] The World Health Organization also advised that, 'Masks should be used as part of a comprehensive strategy of measures to suppress transmission and save lives'.[38]

Nevertheless, questions surrounding the compatibility of requirements to wear masks have been raised before the ECtHR. For example, as noted above, in *Piperea v Romania*,[39] one of the aspects of the state's response to COVID-19 with which the applicant took issue was the requirement to wear a mask. However, the ECtHR pointed out that the measures in question had

32 At para. 51.

33 At para. 54.

34 At para. 59.

35 At para. 63.

36 [2023] NICA 28.

37 World Health Organization, 'Coronavirus disease (COVID-19): Masks', 5 January 2022, https://www.who.int/emergencies/diseases/novel-coronavirus-2019/question-and-answers-hub/q-a-detail/coronavirus-disease-covid-19-masks.

38 World Health Organization, 'Coronavirus disease (COVID-19) advice for the public: When and how to use masks', December 2021, https://www.who.int/emergencies/diseases/novel-coronavirus-2019/advice-for-public/when-and-how-to-use-masks.

39 App. No. 24183/21, decision of 5 July 2022.

been imposed on the entire population due to what the national authorities had regarded as a serious public health situation. The applicant had complained in the abstract that the measures taken by the state had been inadequate and inappropriate and had not provided information about his individual situation or explained in specific terms how he had been directly affected. The ECtHR, therefore, held that the application either did not meet the admissibility criteria set out in Articles 34 and 35 or did not disclose any appearance of a violation of the rights contained in the ECHR.

The issue of the compatibility of requirements to wear masks with the provisions of the ECHR also arose in *Makovetskyy v Ukraine*.[40] On 9 December 2020, the state had adopted measures requiring the wearing of face masks in public buildings and on public transport as part of its response to the COVID-19 pandemic. On 30 December 2020, the applicant in this case entered a supermarket without wearing a mask and then refused to put one on despite a security guard asking him to do so. The police were called, and the applicant was found guilty of an administrative offence for failing to wear a face mask in a public building. A fine of 170 Ukrainian hryvnias, which equated to approximately 4.90 euro, was imposed. The applicant appealed to the domestic courts, arguing that the measure in question had not been legitimate or necessary. However, his appeal was dismissed, and the fine was upheld. As the relevant legislation establishing the measure and liability for non-compliance with the requirement to wear a face mask had been in force at the time in question, it was held that the police officer's actions had been lawful.

The applicant then took a case before the ECtHR, arguing that the administrative offence proceedings were in breach of the right to a fair trial under Article 6 and the principle of no punishment without law under Article 7 of the ECHR. However, the ECtHR found that there was nothing which could lead it to conclude that the domestic courts had acted in an unreasonable or arbitrary way in assessing the evidence, establishing the facts or interpreting the relevant law. The applicant had argued before the domestic courts that the imposition of measures to control the COVID-19 virus, including the requirement to wear a face mask and the subsequent actions of the police, had been unlawful. The domestic courts had examined the applicant's arguments, established that he had committed an administrative offence punishable under the relevant legislation and found against him. There was, thus, no indication that the applicant had been prevented from making his case or that the findings of the domestic courts were manifestly unreasonable or arbitrary. The ECtHR was, thus, of the view that the arguments based on Article 6 were manifestly ill-founded. The ECtHR also held that Article 7 was not applicable, as there had been no criminal charge. The fine had been negligible and

40 App. No. 50824/21, decision of 19 May 2022.

failure to pay could not lead to deprivation of liberty. The application was, therefore, inadmissible.

Although both *Piperea v Romania* and *Makovetskyy v Ukraine* were admissibility decisions, it seems clear from these cases that the ECtHR would not hold that a requirement imposed by a state in response to the pandemic that masks should be worn in public places was in breach of the ECHR. The Court has made it clear that measures imposed on an entire population due to the pandemic will not be held to violate the ECtHR unless the applicant explains in specific terms how they were directly affected. It is very unlikely that an applicant could make a case that a requirement to wear a mask affected them in a sufficient manner so as to fulfil this requirement unless, for example, they had a medical condition making it difficult for them to wear a mask. It is probable, however, that most, if not all, requirements to wear masks would have provided for exemptions in such situations.

Nevertheless, there are currently applications pending before the ECtHR which relate to requirements to wear masks in the context of the pandemic. For example, in *Arus v Romania*,[41] the applicant argues that an obligation to wear a mask in public spaces violated his right to freedom of movement under Article 2 of Protocol No. 4. The pending applications of *Danijel Grgicin v Croatia*[42] and *Liam Grgicin v Croatia*[43] also concern circumstances relating to a requirement to wear masks in the context of the pandemic. On 27 June 2020, the first applicant boarded a train without wearing a protective mask, along with his son, the second applicant, who was at the time two and a half years old. Two days prior to this, an official instruction had come into force stating that all passengers using public transportation were required to wear a mask. The first applicant was requested to put on a mask or leave the train, by both the train personnel and a police officer, but he refused to do so. However, on seeing three more police officers approaching, he then put on a mask. The first applicant was subsequently informed that proceedings would be initiated against him for disturbing the public order and insulting a police officer. As he refused to leave the train, he was apprehended by the police officers, carried off the train and handcuffed. The second applicant, who had witnessed the scene, began to cry. The applicants were brought to the police station where they remained for two hours before being released. They complained to the relevant authorities about the conduct of the police, but their complaint was dismissed as was their subsequent complaint to the Constitutional Court. In minor-offence proceedings, the first applicant was acquitted of the charges of disturbing peace and public order by insulting a police officer. The applicants complain, under Article 3 of the ECHR, that the force used by the police

41 App. No. 39647/21.
42 App. No. 6749/22.
43 App. No. 7154/22.

against the first applicant had been disproportionate and that the investigation into their allegations had not been effective. They also complain that the violent arrest of the first applicant and keeping the second applicant at the police station without anyone taking care of him exposed the second applicant to inhuman and degrading treatment.

Vaccination Requirements

Another type of measure which was adopted in a number of states in response to the pandemic was a requirement for those employed in certain sectors to be vaccinated against COVID-19. For example, in *Zambrano v France* (which was discussed earlier in the chapter),[44] the applicant alluded to the fact that vaccination was compulsory for persons working in the health and social-care sectors, except when such persons had medical reasons for not receiving a COVID-19 vaccine. However, this point was not considered by the ECtHR, as the applicant had not submitted evidence that he worked in such a sector.

The issue of compulsory vaccination for those working in certain sectors was, nevertheless, the central issue in *Thevenon v France*.[45] On 5 August 2021, a law was passed in France which made vaccination against the COVID-19 virus compulsory for workers in the health, emergency and social services sectors, except for those who were medically exempt. The applicant, who was a professional and volunteer firefighter, did not take the vaccine. On 19 August 2021, the applicant, along with other firefighters and a number of hospital employees lodged a request under Rule 39 of the Rules of Court of the ECtHR for the Court to indicate as an interim measure that the vaccination requirement should be suspended. However, on 24 August 2021, the ECtHR denied this request on the grounds that it did not fall within the scope of Rule 39.[46] On 15 September 2021, the applicant was suspended without pay from his duties as a professional firefighter and was also suspended from service as a volunteer firefighter. He did not challenge these orders.

The applicant lodged a complaint to the ECtHR, arguing that his right to respect for private and family life under Article 8, read alone and in conjunction with the prohibition of discrimination under Article 14, and his right to protection of property under Article 1 of Protocol No. 1, had been breached by the vaccination requirement imposed upon him due to his occupation and

44 App. No. 41994/21, decision of 7 October 2021.

45 App. No. 46061/21, decision of 6 October 2022.

46 As was discussed in Chapter 1, under Rule 39 of the Rules of Court of the ECtHR, the Court may indicate interim measures to any state party to the ECHR. These are urgent measures which apply only when there is an imminent risk of irreparable harm. Such measures are decided in connection with proceedings before the ECtHR and do not prejudge any subsequent decisions on the admissibility or merits of the case in question. The Rules of Court of the ECtHR are available at https://www.echr.coe.int/documents/rules_court_eng.pdf.

by his suspension from the fire service without pay by virtue of his refusal to receive the COVID-19 vaccine. However, the ECtHR noted that the applicant had not applied to the French administrative courts for judicial review of the orders which suspended him from his duties as a professional firefighter and from service as a volunteer firefighter, even though he had had a window of two months in which to do so. In French law, an action for judicial review, in which a breach of the ECtHR was a permissible ground on which to rely in support of a claim for a quashing order, was one of the domestic remedies which had to be exhausted. The ECtHR also stated that an appeal on a point of law to the French Court of Cassation, or the *Conseil d'Etat*, ordinarily needed to be pursued if the requirements of Article 35 of the ECtHR were to be met. In general, in order for all domestic remedies to be exhausted, the case had to be litigated, should occasion arise, all the way to the court of final appeal, and the claimant had to place before that court the relevant complaints under the ECHR that may then be brought before the ECtHR. It was, therefore, held that the application was inadmissible due to a failure to exhaust domestic remedies.

It is, however, somewhat unfortunate that the applicant had not exhausted domestic remedies in this instance, as this meant that the substantive issue – the compatibility with the ECHR of compulsory vaccination requirements against COVID-19 for those working in certain occupations – was not considered by the ECtHR. It would certainly have been interesting to obtain the Court's views on this matter, and in the absence of a substantive judgment on the merits of the case, one can only speculate on the views which the ECtHR would have adopted. However, the aim of mandatary vaccination requirements for those working in certain services was to protect the public, including those particularly vulnerable to the COVID-19 virus. Health, emergency and social services sectors are essential services, and in many cases, individuals have little choice but to engage with such services when the need arises. It would, therefore, seem likely that the ECtHR would view mandatory vaccination requirements as constituting a valid restriction on the rights contained, for example, in Article 8 of the ECHR and Article 1 of Protocol No. 1, for the purposes of protecting health and the rights and freedoms of others.

Indeed, although the issue of requirements for compulsory vaccination against COVID-19 for those working in certain sectors has not yet been considered substantively by the ECtHR, the Court has previously accorded substantive consideration to compulsory vaccination requirements, albeit not in the COVID-19 context. As was referred to in Chapter 3, in *Vavřička and Others v. Czech Republic*[47] the Grand Chamber addressed an issue surrounding the imposition of fines on parents and the exclusion of children from preschool due to refusal to comply with a statutory child vaccination duty. In

47 App. Nos. 47621/13, 3867/14, 73094/14, 19298/15, 19306/15 and 43883/15, judgment of 8 April 2021.

its judgment, the Grand Chamber stated that, in principle, matters of public health fall within the margin of appreciation of states and commented that 'the margin of appreciation available to the respondent State is generally wide when it has to strike a balance between competing private and public interests or different rights protected by the Convention'.[48] The Grand Chamber held that the measures imposed due to failure to comply with the duty in question fell within the state's margin of appreciation and, therefore, did not constitute a violation of the right to respect for private and family life under Article 8, the right to freedom of opinion under Article 9 or the right to education under Article 2 of Protocol No. 1. It would seem likely that the ECtHR would adopt a similar approach to compulsory vaccination requirements against COVID-19 for those working in certain occupations and hold that such requirements fall within the margin of appreciation enjoyed by states.

Nevertheless, the issue of the compatibility with the ECHR of compulsory vaccination for those working in certain sectors has again been raised in an application which is currently pending before the ECtHR, so a ruling on this substantive issue may yet be issued by the Court. *Pasquinelli and Others v San Marino*[49] involves 26 applicants who are health care and social health workers employed with the San Marino social security service and other public entities. An obligation to be vaccinated against COVID-19 was imposed by law on their professional sector. They refused to be vaccinated, and, as a result, they were temporarily suspended from their functions without pay. The San Marino Constitutional Court held that the law in question was legitimate and compatible with the San Marino Constitution, the ECHR and other instruments. However, the applicants complain to the ECtHR of a violation of their rights under Article 8 of the ECHR.

Restrictions on Professional Activities

Measures which were adopted by many states in response to the COVID-19 pandemic undoubtedly placed restrictions on the employment and professional activities of individuals, and, indeed, many lost their employment or their businesses.[50] For example, in the admissibility decision of *Toromag, s.r.o and Others v Slovakia*,[51] the applicants were owners of fitness centres which were closed due to measures taken by the Public Health Authority of Slovakia to prevent the spread of COVID-19 during the period from 15

48 At para. 275.
49 App. No. 24622/22.
50 International Labour Organization, 'COVID-19 and the World of Work', https://www.ilo.org/global/topics/coronavirus/lang--en/index.htm.
51 App. Nos. 41217/20, 41253/20, 41263/20, 41271/20 and 49716/20, decision of 25 August 2022.

March 2020 until 19 May 2020. The applicants argued that these measures were unlawful and that their rights under Article 1 of Protocol No. 1[52] were violated due to the alleged pecuniary damage incurred and the loss of future income and clientele. However, the ECtHR held that the applications were inadmissible. Although the applications had been introduced several months after the applicants had lodged complaints before the domestic Constitutional Court, the applicants had stated that they had been unable to have the measures in question reviewed by the domestic courts. In addition, the applicants had failed to inform the ECtHR of the outcome of the constitutional proceedings despite having been advised of the duty to keep the Court informed of all relevant developments. The ECtHR, therefore, concluded that the applicants had deliberately withheld significant information which they had known from the outset and that they had failed to inform the Court regarding significant developments which had occurred during the proceedings. The applications were, thus, inadmissible due to their abusive nature and were rejected in accordance with Article 35(3) and (4) of the ECHR.

Again, it is rather unfortunate that the circumstances of the applications in *Toromag, s.r.o and Others v Slovakia* meant that they were inadmissible, and, therefore, the substantive issue was not considered by the ECtHR. Nevertheless, the measures at issue in *Toromag* were very typical of those which were adopted by many states parties to the ECHR during the early months of the pandemic. In many states, businesses such as fitness centres were closed in order to attempt to limit the spread of the COVID-19 virus. The measures in question applied for only a relatively short period of time – around two months – and it had been possible for them to be reviewed by the domestic Constitutional Court. It is, thus, very likely that the ECtHR would view such measures as constituting a valid restriction on the rights found in Article 1 of Protocol No. 1 for the purposes of protecting health and the rights and freedoms of others.

It is notable that the restrictions on professional activities imposed in the context of the pandemic and their compatibility with the ECHR was considered by the domestic courts in the UK in *R (Dolan) v Secretary of State for Health and Social Care*.[53] As mentioned earlier in the chapter, under the regulations at issue in this case, certain businesses had to close. Under Regulations 4 and 5 as originally formulated, from 26 March 2020, businesses such as restaurants and cafes were prohibited from selling food and drink

52 Article 1 of Protocol No. 1 states that, 'Every natural or legal person is entitled to the peaceful enjoyment of his possessions. No one shall be deprived of his possessions except in the public interest and subject to the conditions provided for by law and by the general principles of international law. The preceding provisions shall not, however, in any way impair the right of a State to enforce such laws as it deems necessary to control the use of property in accordance with the general interest or to secure the payment of taxes or other contributions or penalties'.

53 [2020] EWHC 1786 (Admin); [2020] EWCA Civ 1605.

for consumption on the premises, whilst other businesses and shops were required to close or to cease carrying on business, apart from specified exceptions such as food retailers, pharmacies, banks, petrol stations and newsagents. Following later amendments to the regulations, shops were permitted to open from 15 June 2020. The first appellant in *Dolan* was a British citizen who lived in Monaco and who was the owner of businesses based in the UK. One of these was a public relations company which had seen a decline in revenues. Another was a company which leased planes to airlines such as Air France and British Airways and which had been severely affected during the pandemic. The first appellant argued that his rights under Article 1 of Protocol No. 1 had been violated.

However, the domestic courts were firmly of the view that these circumstances did not give rise to a breach of this provision. As Lewis J. in the High Court stated, 'there is no evidence that the Regulations have deprived the first claimant (or anyone else) of any possessions within the meaning of the Convention'.[54] Lewis J. proceeded to comment that,

> (T)he first claimant has simply not provided sufficient evidence that the Regulations have involved any unlawful interference with his possessions or property such as would justify permitting this claim to proceed. So far as possessions are concerned, existing case law is that this does not include loss of revenue but will include goodwill. So far as the public relations company is concerned, there is evidence that it has lost revenue but no evidence to indicate that the goodwill of the company has suffered.[55]

In relation to the airline leasing business, the first appellant argued that the regulations, which originally prevented people leaving their homes without reasonable excuse and which were then amended to prevent people staying elsewhere overnight, inflicted harm to this business. However, Lewis J. was of the view that 'there is simply no realistic basis on which it could be said that the Regulations have caused the loss or damage to that business'.[56] He proceeded to state that,

> It is overwhelmingly far more likely that the cause of any economic harm to that business is the restrictions on flights imposed by other countries or the fact that people are unable or unwilling to fly to other countries because of restrictions or fears about the situation in those other countries. If inferences are to be drawn, therefore, the overwhelmingly reasonable inference to draw is that any harm to the first claimant's airline leasing

54 [2020] EWHC 1786 (Admin), at para. 101.
55 At para. 102.
56 At para. 103.

> business has been caused by other factors (such as restrictions on flights imposed by other countries or difficulties in travel to other countries) not by the Regulations.[57]

The first appellant also argued that other people, who were not parties in the case, but who ran businesses which were affected by Regulations 4 or 5, may be able to demonstrate a breach of Article 1 of Protocol No. 1. However, in response, Lewis J. asserted that, This court is concerned with the position of the current three claimants and the current evidence before it. It is not appropriate to speculate about who else might bring a claim and what evidence they might be able to produce',[58] and concluded that, 'In all the circumstances, the first claimant has not established an evidential basis that the Regulations have even arguably involved a breach of his rights under Article 1 of the First Protocol'.[59]

The Court of Appeal was firmly in agreement with the judgment of Lewis J. on these points and stated that,

> it is impossible to conceive that there was a disproportionate interference with the right in A1P1. The margin of judgement to be afforded to the executive is particularly wide in this context, because this was a "control of use" case and not a deprivation of property case.[60]

The Court of Appeal likewise concluded, therefore, that there was 'no arguable basis for the contention that there was a breach of A1P1'.[61]

It is not, of course, the case that the ECtHR will always interpret the rights contained in the ECHR in the same way as a domestic court. Indeed, as was discussed in Chapter 3, in *Communauté Genevoise D'Action Syndicale (CGAS) v Switzerland*,[62] the ECtHR adopted an approach to the application of Article 11 to restrictions on public gatherings in the context of the pandemic which was diametrically opposed to that which the UK domestic courts had taken in *Dolan*. Therefore, it cannot automatically be assumed that if considering a case concerning the application of Article 1 of Protocol No. 1 in this context that the ECtHR would adopt the same approach as was taken by the domestic courts in the *Dolan* case. Nevertheless, it is noteworthy that the judgment of Lewis J. does not entirely rule out the possibility that a violation of Article 1 of Protocol No. 1 could be found in a case involving restrictions imposed due to the pandemic. When considering the issue surrounding the

57 At para. 104.
58 At para. 105.
59 At para. 105.
60 [2020] EWCA Civ 1605, at para. 110.
61 At para. 111.
62 App. No. 21881/20, judgment of 15 March 2022.

decline in revenues of the first appellant's public relations company, Lewis J. commented, as noted previously, that whilst 'possessions' does not include revenue, it does include goodwill. Although evidence had been brought to demonstrate that the company in question had lost revenue, no evidence had been adduced to show that the goodwill of the company had suffered. If sufficient evidence had been brought to demonstrate that the goodwill of the company had suffered, this may have established an interference with the peaceful enjoyment of the first appellant's possessions. Likewise, in responding to the argument of the first appellant that other people who ran businesses, but who were not parties in the case, may be able to demonstrate a violation of Article 1 of Protocol No. 1, Lewis J. did not rule out the possibility of others being able to do so but simply stated that it was not appropriate to speculate regarding other potential claims. For example, in *Toromag, s.r.o and Others v Slovakia*, part of the applicants' argument that their rights under Article 1 of Protocol No. 1 had been breached related to the loss of clientele, which would seem to constitute loss of goodwill as referred to by Lewis J. Nevertheless, it must be remembered that, even if measures introduced in response to the pandemic were deemed to constitute a restriction on the peaceful enjoyment of possessions, it is very likely that any such interference would be viewed as being proportionate. Article 1 of Protocol No. 1 itself asserts 'the right of a State to enforce such laws as it deems necessary to control the use of property in accordance with the general interest', and it would certainly appear that 'the general interest' would encompass the necessity of protecting life and public health in the context of the pandemic. Indeed, the Court of Appeal was strongly of the opinion that it was 'impossible to conceive that there was a disproportionate interference'[63] with Article 1 of Protocol No. 1 in these circumstances.

Restrictions in Prisons

As was discussed in Chapter 2, individuals in prisons and other detention facilities were at particular risk of contracting the COVID-19 virus due to being confined in close proximity to large numbers of other persons. It is, therefore, unsurprising that cases have come before the ECtHR in which detainees have argued that insufficient measures were adopted to protect them from the virus.[64] However, conversely, it is also true that certain measures adopted to prevent the spread of COVID-19 had a severe effect on detainees. Given that the freedoms of detainees are, by definition, already restricted considerably, further restrictions imposed as a result of the pandemic had the potential to impact greatly on such individuals. As the World Health Organization stated,

63 [2020] EWCA Civ 1605, at para. 110.
64 For example, *Feilazoo v Malta*, App. No. 6865/19, judgment of 11 March 2021.

> The psychological and behavioural reactions of people in prison or those detained in other settings are likely to differ from those of people who observe physical distancing in the community; consideration should therefore be given to the increased need for emotional and psychological support, for transparent awareness-raising and information-sharing on the disease, and for assurances that continued contact with family and relatives will be upheld.[65]

In March 2020, the European Committee for the Prevention of Torture and Inhuman or Degrading Treatment or Punishment (CPT) issued a statement of principles relating to the treatment of persons deprived of their liberty in the context of the COVID-19 pandemic,[66] in which it emphasised that, 'Protective measures must never result in inhuman or degrading treatment of persons deprived of their liberty'. The CPT proceeded to state that,

> Any restrictive measure taken vis-à-vis persons deprived of their liberty to prevent the spread of Covid-19 should have a legal basis and be necessary, proportionate, respectful of human dignity and restricted in time. Persons deprived of their liberty should receive comprehensive information, in a language they understand, about any such measures.

The statement also asserted that,

> While it is legitimate and reasonable to suspend non-essential activities, the fundamental rights of detained persons during the pandemic must be fully respected. This includes in particular the right to maintain adequate personal hygiene (including access to hot water and soap) and the right of daily access to the open air (of at least one hour). Further, any restrictions on contact with the outside world, including visits, should be compensated for by increased access to alternative means of communication (such as telephone or Voice-over-Internet-Protocol communication).

65 World Health Organization, Regional Office for Europe, 'Preparedness, prevention and control of COVID-19 in prisons and other places of detention', Interim guidance, 8 February 2021, https://www.who.int/europe/publications/i/item/WHO-EURO-2021-1405-41155-57257, at 5. See also HM Inspectorate of Prisoners, 'What happens to prisoners in a pandemic? A thematic review by HM Inspectorate of Prisons', February 2021, https://www.justiceinspectorates.gov.uk/hmiprisons/wp-content/uploads/sites/4/2021/02/What-happens-to-prisoners-in-a-pandemic.pdf.

66 European Committee for the Prevention of Torture and Inhuman or Degrading Treatment or Punishment, 'Statement of principles relating to the treatment of persons deprived of their liberty in the context of the coronavirus disease (Covid-19) pandemic', 20 March 2020, CPT/Inf(2020)13.

The CPT stated that if a detainee is placed in isolation or quarantine due to being infected or suspected of being infected by the COVID-19 virus, the person concerned should be provided with 'meaningful human contact' on a daily basis. Also, 'Fundamental safeguards against the ill-treatment of persons in the custody of law enforcement officials (access to a lawyer, access to a doctor, notification of custody) must be fully respected in all circumstances and at all times'.

The case of *Fenech v Malta*[67] abundantly illustrates the particular difficulties involved with providing an effective response to COVID-19 in the context of prisons. As was discussed in Chapter 2, the applicant, who had been remanded in custody, argued that there had been violations of Articles 2 and 3 on the grounds that sufficient measures had not been taken to protect him from contracting COVID-19. However, he additionally alleged that a number of the measures which had been taken were themselves in breach of Article 3, in that, for a certain period of time, he had had no access to the gym, to his family or to other activities. This case also illustrates the two broad categories into which ECHR claims in the pandemic context fall – those based on arguments that states did not put in place sufficient measures to protect individuals from the virus and those entailing arguments that the measures put in place themselves involved breaches of rights – in that both types of claims were made in this instance.

The ECtHR noted that the limitations in question had occurred within the very specific context of a public health emergency and were put in place in view of significant health considerations. The limitations applied not only to the applicant but to society in general. The Court stated that,

> the Covid-19 pandemic is liable to have very serious consequences not just for health, but also for society, the economy, the functioning of the State and life in general, and that the situation should therefore be characterised as an "exceptional and unforeseeable context".[68]

The ECtHR was, therefore, of the view that,

> the mere fact that for a limited time … the applicant could not use the gym or attend mass (while still having access to a Chaplain) – measures which moreover were applicable to all the prison detainees, and the population at large – cannot be considered to have caused him distress or hardship of an intensity exceeding the unavoidable level of suffering inherent in detention during a pandemic.[69]

67 App. No. 19090/20, judgment of 1 March 2022.
68 At para. 96.
69 At para. 96.

As regards the limitation on the applicant's family contacts, the ECtHR noted that family visits had been suspended to secure the well-being of detainees, and it had not been argued that this measure was not necessary, proportionate or restricted in time. Indeed, after a brief period to make the necessary arrangements, the applicant had been allowed to call his family via skype each week, and he was permitted to phone them regularly throughout the relevant period of time. There had, therefore, been no violation of Article 3 regarding the measures in question

In the case of *Constantin-Lucian Spînu v Romania*,[70] the applicant had been in prison since June 2019. Until February 2020, he had been permitted to leave the prison to attend Adventist Church services. In July 2020, he applied to the prison authorities for permission to attend a service every Saturday; however, his request was denied due to restrictive measures put in place because of the COVID-19 pandemic. The applicant argued that this constituted a violation of his right to freedom of religion under Article 9 of the ECHR.

The ECtHR accepted that the matter in question had amounted to an interference with the applicant's right under Article 9. The issue was, therefore, whether this restriction was legitimate. The Court noted that the interference had been prescribed by domestic legislation which contained provisions allowing restrictions to be placed on day release arrangements for prisoners due to the pandemic. In relation to the legitimate aims relied on by the state, it was accepted by the ECtHR that the measure in question had been taken to protect the health and safety of prisoners and anyone who might come into contact with them and to protect public health in general. The Court noted that the protection of public health was one of the aims listed in Article 9(2) as being capable of warranting a limitation on the freedom to manifest one's religion.[71]

As regards whether the interference had been necessary in a democratic society, the ECtHR pointed out that the limitation on the applicant's right to freedom of religion only affected one dimension of the exercise of that right in that it had concerned only his participation in worship outside the prison at the church. The applicant did not argue that he had been prevented from practising his religion in any other way whilst in prison. The Court noted that attendance at church services had been made subject to particular requirements or, indeed, suspended for all members of the church. The ECtHR was of the view that the changing and unforeseeable nature of the situation involving the pandemic must have posed certain challenges to the prison authorities and that the

70 App. No.29443/20, judgment of 11 October 2022.

71 Article 9(2) of the ECHR states that, 'Freedom to manifest one's religion or beliefs shall be subject only to such limitations as are prescribed by law and are necessary in a democratic society in the interests of public safety, for the protection of public order, health or morals, or for the protection of the rights and freedoms of others'.

authorities should, therefore, be afforded a wide margin of appreciation, particularly as the applicant had been seeking permission to leave the prison and interact with individuals who were not inmates or staff of the prison. The risk of the applicant being infected outside the prison and bringing the virus back into that environment would have carried significant weight in the assessment of the prison authorities. The ECtHR accepted that the authorities had been in a difficult position and alternatives had been offered with the prison introducing the use of videoconferencing for Adventist worship. The Court was of the view that this solution was consistent with the practices which had developed generally during the pandemic and also with the recommendation by the CPT that any restrictions on contact with the outside world should be compensated for by increased access to alternative means of communication.[72] The ECtHR, therefore, held that there had been no violation of Article 9.

There are currently two applications pending before the ECtHR which also raise issues relating to measures imposed in prisons. In *Guhn v Poland*[73] and *Michalski v Poland*,[74] the applicants, who are prisoners, complain about the introduction of restrictive measures relating to the pandemic in prisons and, in particular, they argue that the long-lasting prohibition of family visits in prison violated their right to respect for their private and family life under Article 8 of the ECHR.

Impact on Criminal Proceedings

In addition, there are a number of pending applications before the ECtHR in which arguments are being made that measures adopted due to the pandemic impacted upon criminal proceedings in ways which violated the ECHR. For example, *Khokhlov v Cyprus*[75] concerns the applicant's ongoing detention since October 2018 for the purpose of his extradition to Russia to stand trial. In October 2020, he was informed that, due to measures put in place by Cyprus and Russia in response to the pandemic, the two states had decided to suspend his extradition. The applicant complains, in particular, that he has been unlawfully and arbitrarily deprived of his liberty in violation of Article 5 of the ECHR, the right to liberty, as a result of unjustified delays in effecting his extradition. *Ait Oufella v France*[76] relates to an argument that pre-trial detentions which were extended automatically without any decision of a judge in the context of emergency legislation enacted at the beginning of

72 European Committee for the Prevention of Torture and Inhuman or Degrading Treatment or Punishment, op. cit.
73 App. No. 45519/20.
74 App. No. 34180/20.
75 App. No. 53114/20.
76 App. No. 51860/20.

the pandemic, constituted a breach of Article 5. In *Dumea v Romania*,[77] the applicant complains under Article 6 of the ECHR, the right to a fair trial, in relation to the lack of public access to the courtroom in the context of criminal proceedings due to measures taken in response to the pandemic.

Impact on Asylum Seekers

It has been commented that, 'All over the world, in countries with different migration presence and dynamics, migrants have been disproportionately affected by the pandemic'.[78] It is, therefore, unsurprising that issues have been raised before the ECtHR relating to the impact on asylum seekers of measures adopted by states in response to the COVID-19 pandemic. For example, in *Bah v the Netherlands*,[79] the applicant was a Guinean national whose asylum application in the Netherlands had been rejected and who had been placed in immigration detention with a view to his deportation. On 5 March 2020, the applicant lodged an appeal against the detention order with the Regional Court, which informed him the next day that his hearing was scheduled to take place on 19 March. However, on 15 March, the Council for the Judiciary published an announcement to the effect that, as of 17 March, all Dutch courts would be closed for all but the most urgent cases until 6 April 2020 due to the

77 App. No. 6457/21.

78 Twigg, J., Mathews, R. and Guadagno, L., *Inclusion of Migrants and Refugees in Preparedness and Response to Biological Disasters: Case Study of the COVID-19 Pandemic*, 2022, Council of Europe, https://edoc.coe.int/en/refugees/11301-inclusion-of-migrants-and-refugees-in-preparedness-and-response-to-biological-disasters-case-study-of-the-covid-19-pandemic.html, at 5. See also Iov, C.A., 'The effects of the COVID-19 pandemic on immigrants, refugees and asylum seekers in the European Union: From theory to practice' (2021) 22 *Research and Science Today* 9; Burns, N., Mulvey, G., Piacentini, T. and Vidal, N., 'Refugees, political bounding and the pandemic: Material effects and experiences of categorisations amongst refugees in Scotland' (2022) 48 *Journal of Ethnic and Migration Studies* 4066; Mercier, E. and Rehaag, S., 'The right to seek asylum in Canada (during a global pandemic)' (2020) 57 *Osgoode Hall Law Journal* 705; El Tatary, G. and Gill, N., 'The impact of the COVID-19 pandemic on the mental health and wellbeing of refugees and asylum seekers – A narrative review of the literature' (2022) 30 *Australasian Psychiatry* 728; Libal, K., Harding, S., Popescu, M., Berthold, S.M. and Felten, G., 'Human Rights of Forced Migrants During the COVID-19 Pandemic: An Opportunity for Mobilization and Solidarity' (2021) 6 *Journal of Human Rights and Social Work* 148; Mengesha, Z, Alloun, E., Weber, D., Smith, M. and Harris, P., '"Lived the pandemic twice": A scoping review of the unequal impact of the COVID-19 pandemic on asylum seekers and undocumented migrants' (2022) 18 *International Journal of Environmental Research and Public Health* 6624; Ghezelbash, D. and Tan, N.F., 'The end of the right to seek asylum? COVID-19 and the future of refugee protection' (2020) 32 *International Journal of Refugee Law* 668; Kenny, M.A., Grech, C. and Procter, N. 'A trauma informed response to COVID 19 and the deteriorating mental health of refugees and asylum seekers with insecure status in Australia' (2022) 31 *International Journal of Mental Health Nursing* 62; and Triandafyllidou, A., *Migration and Pandemics*, 2022, Springer International Publishing, Bern.

79 App. No. 35751/20, decision of 22 June 2021.

pandemic. In-person hearings were cancelled, with cases being processed in writing as much as possible. On 18 March 2020, the Regional Court informed the applicant that his appeal could be heard on the scheduled date in writing or by teleconference and that only his lawyer would be able to join. It would not be possible for the applicant to attend the hearing in person or to be heard by tele- or videoconferencing due to infrastructure problems at the beginning of the pandemic. On 30 March, the applicant's appeal was dismissed by the Regional Court.

The applicant argued that his right to liberty under Article 5 of the ECHR had been breached, as he had not been heard in person by the Regional Court regarding his immigration detention order. The applicant submitted that the special measures implemented as a result of the COVID-19 pandemic did not justify his not having been heard in person on the lawfulness of his detention. He also argued that he should have been immediately released from immigration detention when it became apparent that he could not be heard in person by the Regional Court. The ECtHR noted, however, that the applicant had benefitted from adversarial proceedings during which he had been assisted by a lawyer who had made submissions in writing on his behalf and attended the hearing of 19 March 2020 by telephone. The hearing had taken place during the first weeks of the lockdown in the Netherlands, at which time immigration detention centres were largely unprepared to observe the required social distancing of 1.5 metres in tele- and videoconference rooms. The ECtHR was, therefore, of the view that,

> Given the difficult and unforeseen practical problems with which the State was confronted during the first weeks of the Covid-19 pandemic, the fact that the applicant was represented by and heard through his lawyer with whom he had regular contact and who presented his views on his behalf, the importance of the applicant's other applicable fundamental rights and the general interest of public health…it was not incompatible with Article 5 § 4 to assess the applicant's detention order without securing his attendance at the hearing in person or by videoconference.[80]

The Court thus held that the application was inadmissible as being manifestly ill-founded.

E.B. v Serbia[81] and *A.A. v Serbia*[82] are pending applications which concern a temporary restriction on freedom of movement, between 1 March and 14 May 2020, of refugees, asylum seekers and migrants accommodated in asylum and reception centres in Serbia. The applicants, who are asylum

80 At para. 44.
81 App. No. 50086/20.
82 App. No. 50898/20.

seekers, argue that the de facto 24-hour lockdown in the asylum centre in which they had been staying was tantamount to house arrest and, therefore, constituted an unlawful, arbitrary, unnecessary and collective deprivation of liberty in violation of Article 5. The applicants argue that the contested measures were imposed on the basis of discriminatory criteria, in breach of the Article 14 non-discrimination provision, as they unjustifiably distinguished between refugees, asylum seekers and migrants accommodated in asylum and reception centres and the general population of Serbia and asylum seekers residing in private accommodation. In particular, Serbia was not under general lockdown at the time in question. Rather, the population had freedom of movement, and restaurants, cafes, shopping malls, gyms and other services remained open during all or part of the relevant time period. The applicant in *E.B.* also argues that the measures in question were in contravention of her right to freedom of movement under Article 2 of Protocol No. 4. As a result of these measures, she and her husband both lost their jobs, her two sons could not attend school and the family suffered both physically and mentally, as they were not permitted to go out to purchase essentials for daily life.

Statements on Social Media Regarding the Pandemic

Another type of argument which has been raised before the ECtHR in the context of the COVID-19 pandemic relates to statements concerning the pandemic made by applicants on social media. The pending application of *Avagyan v Russia*[83] concerns a statement made by the applicant in an Instagram post on 13 May 2020 to the effect that there had not been any cases of COVID-19 in a particular region and alleging that money had been offered for agreeing to list COVID-19 as a cause of death on death certificates. On 18 May 2020, the applicant was charged with an offence of disseminating untrue information on the internet. On 8 June 2020, she was found liable for disseminating untrue information and was sentenced to a fine. On 8 July 2020, the District Court dismissed her appeal, referring to regional regulations for preventing the spread of the COVID-19 virus. The applicant argues that her right to freedom of expression under Article 10 of the ECHR was violated, as the law failed to distinguish between dissemination of untrue information and sharing value judgments, that her opinion was based on other internet publications and posed no risk to public health or security and that the amount of the fine was excessive.

In the pending application of *Jeremejevs v Latvia*,[84] the applicant, who is a social and political activist who regularly posts on social media, was placed in detention and subjected to criminal investigation and security measures due to

83 App. No. 36911/20.
84 App. No. 44644/21.

videos which he had posted on Facebook. These videos contained interviews which the applicant had carried out with health care professionals on the subject of COVID-19 and the measures which the Latvian government had implemented to prevent and control the spread of the virus. A criminal investigation in relation to the offence of hooliganism had commenced in December 2020, and the applicant's subsequent requests to terminate the proceedings had been dismissed. As in *Avagyan v Russia*, the applicant likewise argues that his Article 10 right has been violated.

Petrova v Bulgaria[85] also relates to a statement made by the applicant on Facebook. From 13 March 2020, various restrictions were imposed in Bulgaria with the aim of preventing or limiting the spread of the COVID-19 virus. These measures included a prohibition on visits to restaurants, bars and similar establishments; an order to all employers to introduce remote working to the extent which was compatible with the nature of the work in question; and a ban on any organised meetings. On 14 May 2020, the restrictions were reduced to encompass only closed spaces in restaurants, bars and similar establishments, and henceforth, only organised meetings which involved in excess of 10 people were banned. Due to the restrictions, the applicant, who worked as a restaurant waitress, was placed on unpaid leave from 14 March 2020 onward. On 8 April 2020, the applicant emailed a letter to various media in which she asked about the parameters of the no-interest loans promised by the authorities in relation to the restrictions which had been imposed and complained about the financial impact of these restrictions. She then proceeded to post the letter on her Facebook wall, allowing public access to the post. On 9 April, the applicant posted a video on Facebook, adding a link to her post of the previous day. In that video, she asked why there was no financial support in Bulgaria, or at least no-interest loans, for people who had been forced to pause working or who had lost their jobs as a result of the COVID-19 restrictions. She asserted that if she did not receive answers by the end of the week, she would go out to protest, whilst wearing a mask and gloves, and called upon others to do likewise. On 10 April, the applicant posted on her Facebook wall, again allowing public access to the post, that at 11:00 a.m. on 13 April, she would go out to protest, whilst wearing a mask and gloves and maintaining distancing, and invited anyone who wished to join her to do so. On 11 April, the applicant wrote another post on her Facebook wall in which she shared a call from someone else for a march at 1:00 p.m. on 13 April to protest against the measures which had been put in place in Bulgaria as a result of the pandemic. The call asked would-be participants to hold the march by moving in a single line and by maintaining a distance of two to three metres from each other. At 9.45 a.m. on 13 April, police officers arrived at the applicant's home and admonished her in writing not to infringe the measures which had

85 App. No. 938/21.

been put in place to prevent the spread of the COVID-19 virus and informed her that doing so was punishable with a term of imprisonment of up to three years. The police officers also served on the applicant a summons for a police interview at 11:00 a.m. the same day. The applicant stated that she could not go to the police station at 11:00 a.m., but she, nevertheless, appeared for the interview at that time. The police officers then showed her the Facebook post of 11 April and asked her to provide explanations about the protest which she was planning. The applicant argues that her rights under Articles 10 and 11 of the ECHR were violated, as the police had admonished her not to go out to protest, summoned her for an interview at the precise time when she had stated that she would go out to protest and opened a criminal investigation.

Conclusion

In conclusion, therefore, this chapter has demonstrated the myriad of issues beyond those relating to restrictions on public gatherings, which have been raised before the ECHR regarding restrictions put in place due to the COVID-19 pandemic. These issues relate to lockdown measures, restrictions on schools, 'health pass' systems, requirements to wear face coverings, requirements for those employed in certain sectors to be vaccinated against COVID-19 and other measures which impacted upon employment and professional activity. In addition, the implementation of protective measures against COVID-19 in respect of prisoners and detainees raised human rights issues for such persons and, in some instances, had an impact upon criminal proceedings. In certain cases, measures adopted in the context of the pandemic also raised particular issues for asylum seekers.

It has been commented in relation to the UK that, 'The government's initial response to the SARS-CoV-2 pandemic collectively constitutes what is probably the most pervasive interference with civil liberties in the UK's history – without doubt the biggest since the ratification of the European Convention on Human Rights'.[86] The same statement could doubtless be made in respect of the responses of most, if not all, states within the Council of Europe to the pandemic. It is, therefore, unsurprising that such a wide range of issues have arisen before the ECtHR in relation to such responses. As discussed in this chapter, decisions have been made by the ECtHR in many of these cases, and it remains to be seen how the Court will approach the questions raised in those which remain pending at the time of writing.

86 McGrogan, op. cit., at p.671.

5 Conclusions

This book has aimed to contribute to the emerging body of literature on human rights and the COVID-19 pandemic by providing detailed analysis of the applicability of the provisions of the ECHR to issues raised by the pandemic and the approaches of the ECtHR to such issues. These are important questions in themselves; however, they may also have implications for the future, as it is very likely that further pandemics will occur.[1] It is, thus, likely that questions similar to those which have arisen concerning the applicability of human rights law generally, and the ECHR more specifically, to issues surrounding the COVID-19 pandemic will arise again in the future.

As was noted in Chapter 1, in March/April 2020, ten states parties to the ECHR chose to enter derogations under Article 15 in respect of the measures which they were adopting due to the pandemic.[2] However, the large majority of the states' parties to the ECHR chose not to enter derogations regarding the measures which they took in response to COVID-19. A number of the rights found in the ECHR can be limited in certain circumstances. For example, with regard to the right to respect for private and family life under Article 8(1), Article 8(2) states that, 'There shall be no interference by a public authority with the exercise of this right except such as is in accordance with the law and is necessary in a democratic society' for a range of reasons including 'the protection of health' and 'the protection of the rights and freedoms of others'. Likewise, the rights contained in Articles 9,[3] 10[4] and 11[5] can all be

1 Marani, M., Katul, G.G., Pan, W.K and Parolari, A.J., 'Intensity and frequency of extreme novel epidemics', 23 August 2021, *Proceedings of the National Academy of Sciences*, https://www.pnas.org/doi/10.1073/pnas.2105482118.

2 The states in question were Albania, Armenia, Estonia, Georgia, Latvia, North Macedonia, the Republic of Moldova, Romania, San Marino and Serbia. Under Article 15(1), 'In time of war or other public emergency threatening the life of the nation any High Contracting Party may take measures derogating from its obligations under this Convention to the extent strictly required by the exigencies of the situation, provided that such measures are not inconsistent with its other obligations under international law'.

3 Article 9 is the right to freedom of thought, conscience and religion.

4 Article 10 is the right to freedom of expression.

5 Article 11 is the right to freedom of assembly and association.

DOI: 10.4324/9781003383437-5

restricted for reasons including protecting health and protecting the rights and freedoms of others. It appears that the states which did not enter derogations chose to rely on such clauses. Nevertheless, it is not clear where the line is drawn between a permissible restriction under a limitation clause and a matter which would require a derogation to be entered. It seems, however, that when assessing measures adopted by states in response to the pandemic, the ECtHR may afford a wider margin of appreciation to states which entered derogations than to those which did not. As was discussed in Chapter 3, there is support for this conclusion in the judgment of the ECtHR in *Communauté Genevoise D'Action Syndicale (CGAS) v Switzerland*,[6] in which the Court referred to the fact that Switzerland had not entered a derogation to Article 11 and was obliged to comply fully with this provision, within the margin of appreciation afforded to it. In any event, issues surrounding measures adopted by states parties in response to the pandemic and their compliance with the ECHR do not hinge on the question of whether they restricted the rights therein, but, rather, they relate to the question of whether these restrictions were legitimate.

As discussed throughout this book, human rights claims in the context of the pandemic fall into two broad categories: those based on arguments that states did not put in place sufficient measures to protect individuals from the virus and those entailing arguments that the measures put in place themselves involved breaches of rights. The essential question with which the ECtHR must grapple is how to adjudicate on the correct balance which should have been struck. The structure of the book has reflected this, in that Chapter 2 addressed the obligations of the state to provide protection from COVID-19, whilst Chapters 3 and 4 proceeded to address the human rights implications of the measures which were put in place to this end.

As was discussed in Chapter 2, the adoption of measures to prevent and limit the spread of the COVID-19 virus was essential in order for states to comply with their positive obligations to protect the right to life as found in Article 2 of the ECHR and the right to be free from torture or inhuman or degrading treatment as found in Article 3. These duties were particularly pertinent in respect of persons who were clinically vulnerable to the virus, such as those who were elderly or who had underlying health conditions. However, there were other categories of individuals who were also at greater risk from COVID-19, due to their circumstances, such as those in detention facilities, and toward whom states, therefore, had particular duties to ensure that their rights under Articles 2 and 3 were not violated in the context of the pandemic. Chapter 2 examined decisions of the ECtHR relating to claims that states did not adopt sufficient measures to provide adequate protection against

6 App. No. 21881/20, judgment of 15 March 2022.

COVID-19, such as *Feilazoo v Malta*,[7] *Fenech v Malta*[8] and *Le Mailloux v France*.[9] In addition, there are currently a number of pending applications relating to such claims.[10] Almost all of the cases in which applicants argue that states have not adopted sufficient protective measures against COVID-19 involve conditions of detention. This is not surprising, given the particular vulnerability of detainees during the pandemic. Such cases tend to relate to particular circumstances in certain facilities and are, therefore, of very specific application.

However, there is a second category of ECHR claims in the context of the pandemic. Rather than entailing arguments that states did not put in place sufficient measures to protect individuals from the virus, this category of cases involves arguments that the measures put in place to this end themselves involved violations of rights. In these instances, applicants argue that general measures adopted by states during the early months of the pandemic to prevent the spread of the virus were in breach of the ECHR. It is certainly not disputed that such measures had a very substantial impact on the lives of individuals. Such measures involved considerable limitations on the rights of individuals under provisions such as the right to respect for private and family life under Article 8; the right to freedom of thought, conscience and religion under Article 9; the right to freedom of expression under Article 10; the right to freedom of assembly and association under Article 11; and the right to freedom of movement under Article 2 of Protocol No. 4. However, it must be remembered that states were taking measures to protect the lives of their citizens from a deadly new virus about which little was known, against which there was no vaccine and for which very few treatments were available. It is submitted that this is an area in which a wide margin of appreciation should be afforded to states. In order to preserve the legitimacy of human rights law, the ECtHR must strike the correct balance between holding states to account for clear breaches of the ECHR, as it quite rightly did in *Feilazoo*, as was highlighted in Chapter 2, but also being cautious of finding violations in cases involving public restrictions which were applied for the purpose of protecting life and health in response to a global pandemic.

As was discussed in Chapter 3, generally one of the most prominent aspects of the responses of states to the pandemic was to put in place measures prohibiting or restricting public gatherings. Such measures raise issues regarding,

7 App. No. 6865/19, judgment of 11 March 2021.

8 App. No. 19090/20, judgment of 1 March 2022.

9 App. No. 18108/20, decision of 5 November 2020.

10 For example, *Maratsis and Others v Greece*, App. No. 39335/20; *Vasilakis and Others v Greece*, App. No. 30379/20; *Vlamis and Others v Greece*, App. Nos. 29655/20, 29689/20, 30240/20, 30418/20 and 30574/20; *Rus v Romania*, App. No. 2621/21; *Riela v Italy*, App. No. 17378/20; *Faia v Italy*, App. No. 17222/20; *Hafeez v the United Kingdom*, App. No. 14198/20; and *Krstic v Serbia*, App. No. 35246/21.

in particular, the right to freedom of assembly and association under Article 11 of the ECHR, as demonstrated in the case of *Communauté Genevoise D'Action Syndicale (CGAS) v Switzerland*,[11] which was considered in detail in Chapter 3. However, as was asserted in this chapter, the finding of a breach of Article 11 in this case was arguably problematic. It has been established by the ECtHR that when there is no consensus among states parties, a wider margin of appreciation should be afforded. There was no consensus among states parties against the type of measure at issue in *CGAS* – indeed, the measure seems to have been very much in line with those imposed by many other states in Europe and elsewhere. The *CGAS* case has, however, been referred to the Grand Chamber, and it remains to be seen whether the apparent problems with the first instance judgment of the ECtHR in this case will be remedied by the judgment of the Grand Chamber. As was also discussed in Chapter 3, there are currently a number of applications pending before the ECtHR which raise similar issues to those considered in *CGAS*.[12] However, with its judgment in this case, the ECtHR may have already embarked upon a problematic course from which retreat may be difficult unless the Grand Chamber ultimately reverses the first instance ruling. In addition, the chapter noted that prior to the judgment of the ECtHR in *CGAS*, the compatibility with Article 11 of restrictions on public gatherings in the context of the pandemic had been considered by the domestic courts in the UK in in *R (Dolan) v Secretary of State for Health and Social Care*.[13] In this case, in discussing the compatibility with Article 11 of broadly similar measures to those at issue in *CGAS*, the UK courts adopted a position which was diametrically opposed to the approach later taken by the ECtHR in the *CGAS* case.

The measures adopted by states in response to the COVID-19 pandemic were not, of course, limited to restrictions on public gatherings; rather, they impacted upon the lives of individuals in a wide range of other ways which also engaged various provisions of the ECHR and in relation to which issues have been raised before the ECtHR, as was discussed in Chapter 4. For example, in *Terhes v Romania*,[14] it was established that lockdown measures did not violate the right to liberty under Article 5 of the ECHR. Although arguments concerning whether restrictions on leaving home breached provisions such as the right to respect for private and family life under Article 8 of the ECHR and the right to freedom of movement under Article 2 of Protocol No. 4 were

11 App. No. 21881/20, judgment of 15 March 2022.

12 *Central Unitaria de Traballadores/as v Spain*, App. No. 49363/20; *Jarocki v Poland*, App. No. 39750/20; *Nemytov v Russia*, App. No. 1257/21; *Azar v* Russia, App. No. 3244/21; and *Kostyukhin v Russia*, App. No. 24699/21.

13 [2020] EWHC 1786 (Admin); [2020] EWCA Civ 1605.

14 App. No. 49933/20, decision of 20 May 2021.

raised in *Piperea v Romania*[15] and *Magdic v Croatia*,[16] the ECtHR did not rule on these substantive issues due to the applications being declared inadmissible, as the applicants had not demonstrated victim status. If seeking to bring a complaint before the ECtHR regarding state responses to the COVID-19 pandemic, an applicant must be extremely careful to explain how any alleged violations of the ECHR affected them at an individual level.[17] Under Article 34 of the ECHR, in order to have standing to take a case, an individual must show that they were 'directly affected' by the measure in question.[18] In the context of restrictions implemented by states in the context of the pandemic, it is, thus, insufficient simply to allege a violation of an ECHR right due to the adoption of a general measure affecting the whole population. Instead, an applicant must provide the ECtHR with precise evidence and facts, explain why they are of the opinion that the provision on which they are relying has been violated and specify in exact terms how the measure in question affected them at a personal level.

As was also discussed in Chapter 4, the compatibility with various provisions of the ECHR of the lockdown regulations imposed in England in response to the pandemic was examined by the domestic courts in the UK in *Dolan*. Although in relation to questions surrounding the application of Article 11 to prohibitions on restrictions on public gatherings, the UK courts in *Dolan* took an approach which seemed to be diametrically opposed to that which was later adopted by the ECtHR in *CGAS*; both the UK courts and the ECtHR are in agreement that lockdown restrictions did not breach Article 5. The UK has not ratified Protocol No. 4; thus, the right to freedom of movement has not been incorporated into UK law by the Human Rights Act 1998 and could not be relied upon by the appellants in *Dolan*. However, as well as relying on Article 5, the appellants argued that the lockdown measures violated Article 8, an argument which was rejected. As noted above, the ECtHR has not yet made a substantive ruling on the compatibility of lockdown measures with Article 8 or, indeed, with Article 2 of Protocol No. 4. It remains to be seen how the ECtHR would approach a case raising such issues in which an applicant has demonstrated the necessary standing to take such a case.

Another common feature of the measures adopted by states in response to the pandemic involved schools being required to teach pupils, partly or wholly, through online methods as opposed to in-person classes. In the

15 App. No. 24183/21, decision of 5 July 2022.
16 App. No. 17578/20, decision of 5 July 2022.
17 See also *Le Mailloux v France*, App. No. 18108/20, decision of 5 November 2020;
18 Article 34 states that, 'The Court may receive applications from any person, nongovernmental organisation or group of individuals claiming to be the victim of a violation by one of the High Contracting Parties of the rights set forth in the Convention or the Protocols thereto. The High Contracting Parties undertake not to hinder in any way the effective exercise of this right'.

pending application of *M.C.K. and M.H.K.-B. and Others v Germany*,[19] the applicants are pupils who attended schools which had been subject to such requirements and who argue that these restrictions breached their rights under Article 8 of the ECHR and Article 2 of Protocol No. 1, which is the right to education. Although the ECtHR has not yet made a ruling in this case, similar requirements were considered by the Court of Appeal of England and Wales in *Dolan*.[20] As was discussed in Chapter 4, the Court of Appeal appeared to be of the opinion that the measures at issue, placing restrictions on schools, did not actually restrict the right to education and that this right would only have been restricted if schools had to close in the sense that all education had to cease. Nevertheless, even if a more expansive approach to the right to education were to be adopted by the ECtHR in *M.C.K. and M.H.K.-B. and Others*, it is very likely that the Court would be of the view that the measures in question constituted proportionate restrictions on this right. Given that school settings generally involve large numbers of pupils in very close contact, it would appear that a move to online learning in the circumstances of the pandemic constituted a proportionate measure with the legitimate aims of protecting life and health.

As lockdown measures eased, many states imposed a 'health pass' system as an interim stage between lockdown and full easing of the COVID-19 restrictions. Under such systems, individuals were typically required to show proof of vaccination against COVID-19, proof of having recently recovered from the virus or evidence of having tested negative for COVID-19 in order to enter certain premises such as restaurants and other hospitality venues. The compatibility of such measures with the provisions of the ECHR was the subject of *Zambrano v France*.[21] Although *Zambrano* was an admissibility decision, as opposed to a full judgment of the ECtHR, the case, nonetheless, indicates that 'health pass' systems will not be deemed to breach the provisions of the ECHR. Given that the aims of such systems were to protect the lives and health of individuals from the COVID-19 virus, it appears that this is the correct approach.

Additionally, during the pandemic, many states imposed requirements to wear face coverings when in indoor public settings, such as shops, as a way of limiting the spread of the virus. Questions surrounding the compatibility of requirements to wear masks have been raised before the ECtHR in *Piperea v Romania*[22] and *Makovetskyy v Ukraine*.[23] Although both *Piperea* and *Makovetskyy* were admissibility decisions, it seems clear from these

19 App. No. 26657/22.

20 [2020] EWCA Civ 1605.

21 App. No. 41994/21, decision of 7 October 2021.

22 App. No. 24183/21, decision of 5 July 2022.

23 App. No. 50824/21, decision of 19 May 2022. See also the pending applications of *Arus v Romania* App. No. 39647/21; *Danijel Grgicin v Croatia*, App. No. 6749/22; and *Liam Grgicin v*

cases that the ECtHR would not hold that a requirement imposed by a state in response to the pandemic that face coverings should be worn was in violation of the ECHR. The Court has made it clear that measures imposed on an entire population due to the pandemic will not be held to breach the ECtHR unless the applicant explains in specific terms how they were directly affected. It is very unlikely that an applicant could make a case that a requirement to wear a mask affected them in a sufficient manner so as to fulfil this requirement, unless they, for example, had a medical condition making it difficult for them to wear a mask. It is probable, however, that most, if not all, requirements to wear masks would have provided for exemptions in such situations.

Another type of measure which was adopted in a number of states in response to the pandemic was a requirement for those employed in certain sectors to be vaccinated against COVID-19. For example, in *Thevenon v France*,[24] the applicant argued that his rights under Articles 8 and 14[25] of the ECHR and Article 1 of Protocol No. 1[26] had been breached by his suspension from the fire service without pay due to his refusal to be vaccinated against COVID-19.[27] It was held, however, that the application was inadmissible due to a failure to exhaust domestic remedies. Nevertheless, the aim of mandatory vaccination requirements for those working in certain services was to protect the public, including those particularly vulnerable to the COVID-19 virus. Health, emergency and social services sectors are essential services, and in many cases, individuals have little choice but to engage with such services when the need arises. It would, thus, appear likely that the ECtHR would view mandatory vaccination requirements as constituting a valid restriction on the rights contained, for example, in Article 8 of the ECHR and Article 1 of Protocol No. 1 for the purposes of protecting health and the rights and freedoms of others.

Indeed, although the issue of requirements for compulsory vaccination against COVID-19 for those working in certain sectors has not yet been considered substantively by the ECtHR, the Court has previously accorded substantive consideration to compulsory vaccination requirements, albeit not in the COVID-19 context. In *Vavřička and Others v. Czech Republic*[28] the Grand Chamber addressed an issue surrounding the imposition of fines on parents and the exclusion of children from preschool due to refusal to comply

---

Croatia, App. No. 7154/22, all of which concern circumstances relating to requirements to wear masks in the context of the pandemic.

24 App. No. 46061/21.

25 Article 14 is the non-discrimination provision.

26 Article 1 of Protocol No. 1 is the right to protection of property.

27 See also the pending application of *Pasquinelli and Others v San Marino*, App. No. 24622/22, in which similar issues are raised.

28 App. Nos. 47621/13, 3867/14, 73094/14, 19298/15, 19306/15 and 43883/15, judgment of 8 April 2021.

with a statutory child vaccination duty. In its judgment, the Grand Chamber stated that, in principle, matters of public health fall within the margin of appreciation of states and asserted that 'the margin of appreciation available to the respondent State is generally wide when it has to strike a balance between competing private and public interests or different rights protected by the Convention'.[29] The Grand Chamber held that the measures imposed due to failure to comply with the duty in question fell within the state's margin of appreciation and, therefore, did not constitute a violation of the right to respect for private and family life under Article 8, the right to freedom of opinion under Article 9 or the right to education under Article 2 of Protocol No. 1. It would appear likely that the ECtHR would adopt a similar approach to compulsory vaccination requirements against COVID-19 for those working in certain occupations and hold that such requirements fall within the margin of appreciation enjoyed by states.

Other measures adopted in response to the pandemic also impacted upon individuals in relation to their employment and professional activity. For example, in *Toromag, s.r.o and Others v Slovakia*,[30] the applicants were owners of fitness centres which were closed due to measures taken to prevent the spread of COVID-19. They argued that their rights under Article 1 of Protocol No. 1 were violated due to the alleged pecuniary damage incurred and the loss of future income and clientele. The ECtHR ultimately held that the applications were inadmissible, as the applicants had deliberately withheld significant information which they had known from the outset and had failed to inform the Court regarding significant developments which had occurred during the proceedings.

However, the compatibility with the ECHR of restrictions on professional activities imposed in the context of the pandemic was considered by the UK domestic courts in *Dolan.* As noted in Chapter 4, under the regulations[31] at issue in this case, certain businesses had to close. Under Regulations 4 and 5 as originally formulated, from 26 March 2020, businesses such as restaurants and cafes were prohibited from selling food and drink for consumption on the premises, whilst other businesses and shops were required to close or to cease carrying on business apart from specified exceptions such as food retailers, pharmacies, banks, petrol stations and newsagents. Following later amendments to the regulations, shops were permitted to open from 15 June 2020. The first appellant in *Dolan* owned a public relations company which had seen a decline in revenues; also, a company which leased planes to airlines such as Air France and British Airways had been severely affected during the

29 At para. 275.

30 App. Nos. 41217/20, 41253/20, 41263/20, 41271/20 and 49716/20.

31 The Health Protection (Coronavirus, Restrictions) (England) Regulations (SI 2020/350).

pandemic. The first appellant argued that his rights under Article 1 of Protocol No. 1 had been breached. However, the UK courts were of the opinion that these circumstances did not give rise to a violation of this provision, with Lewis J. in the High Court stating that there was no evidence that the regulations had deprived the first appellant of his possessions.[32] Lewis J. proceeded to comment that,

> So far as possessions are concerned, existing case law is that this does not include loss of revenue but will include goodwill. So far as the public relations company is concerned, there is evidence that it has lost revenue but no evidence to indicate that the goodwill of the company has suffered.[33]

As regards the airline leasing business, the first appellant argued that the regulations which originally prevented people leaving their homes without reasonable excuse and which were then amended to prevent people staying elsewhere overnight inflicted harm to this business. However, Lewis J. was of the opinion that 'there is simply no realistic basis on which it could be said that the Regulations have caused the loss or damage to that business'.[34] The first appellant also argued that other people, who were not parties in the case but who ran businesses which were affected by Regulations 4 or 5, may be able to demonstrate a violation of Article 1 of Protocol No. 1. However, in response, Lewis J. stated that,

> This court is concerned with the position of the current three claimants and the current evidence before it. It is not appropriate to speculate about who else might bring a claim and what evidence they might be able to produce.[35]

It cannot, of course, automatically be assumed that if considering a case concerning the application of Article 1 of Protocol No. 1 in this context, the ECtHR would adopt the same approach as was taken by the UK courts in *Dolan*. Nevertheless, it is noteworthy that the judgment of Lewis J. does not entirely rule out the possibility that a violation of Article 1 of Protocol No. 1 could be found in a case involving restrictions imposed due to the pandemic. When considering the issue surrounding the decline in revenues of the first appellant's public relations company, Lewis J. remarked, as noted previously, that whilst 'possessions' does not include revenue, it does include goodwill. Although evidence had been brought to show that the company in

32 [2020] EWHC 1786 (Admin), at para. 101.
33 At para. 102.
34 At para. 103.
35 At para. 105.

question had lost revenue, no evidence had been adduced to demonstrate that the goodwill of the company had suffered. If sufficient evidence had been brought to show that the goodwill of the company had suffered, this may have established an interference with the peaceful enjoyment of the first appellant's possessions. Likewise, in responding to the argument of the first appellant that other people who ran businesses but were not parties in the case may be able to demonstrate a violation of Article 1 of Protocol No. 1, Lewis J. did not rule out the possibility of others being able to do so but stated only that it was inappropriate to speculate in relation to other potential claims. For instance, in *Toromag, s.r.o and Others v Slovakia*, part of the applicants' argument that their rights under Article 1 of Protocol No. 1 had been violated related to the loss of clientele, which would appear to constitute loss of goodwill as referred to by Lewis J. Nevertheless, it must be remembered that, even if measures introduced in response to the pandemic were viewed as amounting to a restriction on the peaceful enjoyment of possessions, it is very likely that any such interference would be regarded as being proportionate. Article 1 of Protocol No. 1 itself asserts 'the right of a State to enforce such laws as it deems necessary to control the use of property in accordance with the general interest', and it would certainly appear that 'the general interest' would encompass the necessity of protecting life and public health in the context of the pandemic. Indeed, the Court of Appeal in *Dolan* was strongly of the opinion that it was 'impossible to conceive that there was a disproportionate interference'[36] with Article 1 of Protocol No. 1 in these circumstances.

In addition, whilst states had particular duties under Articles 2 and 3 to adopt protective measures against COVID-19 in respect of prisoners and detainees, as was discussed in Chapter 2, it is also the case that measures adopted to prevent the spread of the virus raised particular human rights issues for such persons. In this context, the case of *Fenech v Malta*[37] abundantly illustrates the two broad categories into which ECHR claims fall – those based on arguments that states did not put in place sufficient measures to protect individuals from the virus and those entailing arguments that the measures put in place themselves involved breaches of rights – in that both types of claims were made in this instance. The applicant, who had been remanded in custody argued that there had been violations of Articles 2 and 3 on the grounds that sufficient measures had not been taken to protect him from contracting COVID-19. Nevertheless, as was discussed in Chapter 4, he also alleged that a number of the measures which had been taken were themselves in breach of Article 3, in that for a certain period of time, he had had no access to the gym, to his family or to other activities; however, no violation of Article 3 was

36 [2020] EWCA Civ 1605, at para. 110.
37 App. No. 19090/20, judgment of 1 March 2022.

found. In *Constantin-Lucian Spînu v Romania*,[38] the applicant had been prevented from leaving prison to attend Adventist Church services due to restrictive measures put in place in response to the pandemic. He complained that this constituted a violation of his right to freedom of religion under Article 9, an argument which was not upheld by the ECtHR. There are also currently two applications pending before the Court which raise issues relating to measures imposed in prisons due to the pandemic. In *Guhn v Poland*[39] and *Michalski v Poland*,[40] the applicants, who are prisoners, complain about the introduction of restrictive measures in prisons, and, in particular, they argue that the long-lasting prohibition of family visits in prison violated their right to respect for their private and family life under Article 8. In addition, there are currently a number of pending applications in which arguments are being made that measures adopted in response to the pandemic impacted upon criminal proceedings in ways which violated the ECHR.[41]

As was also discussed in Chapter 4, issues have been raised before the ECtHR relating to the impact on asylum seekers of measures adopted by states due to the pandemic. For example, in the admissibility decision of *Bah v the Netherlands*,[42] a detainee argued that his Article 5[43] right had been breached, as it had been impossible for him to attend his immigration detention appeal in person due to measures adopted in response to the pandemic or to be heard by tele- or videoconferencing due to infrastructure problems at the beginning of the pandemic. Also, *E.B. v Serbia*[44] and *A.A. v Serbia*[45] are pending applications which concern a temporary restriction on freedom of movement, between 1 March and 14 May 2020, of refugees, asylum seekers and migrants accommodated in asylum and reception centres in Serbia. The applicants, who are asylum seekers, argue that the de facto 24-hour lockdown in the asylum centre in which they had been staying was tantamount to house arrest and, therefore, constituted an unlawful, arbitrary, unnecessary and collective deprivation of liberty in violation of Article 5. The applicants also argue that the contested measures were imposed on the basis of discriminatory criteria, in breach of the Article 14 non-discrimination provision, as they unjustifiably distinguished between refugees, asylum seekers and migrants accommodated in asylum and reception centres and the general population of Serbia and asylum seekers residing in private accommodation.

38 App. No.29443/20), judgment of 11 October 2022.
39 App. No. 45519/20.
40 App. No. 34180/20.
41 *Khokhlov v Cyprus*, App. No. 53114/20; *Ait Oufella v France*, App. No. 51860/20; and *Dumea v Romania*, App. No. 6457/21.
42 App. No. 35751/20, decision of 22 June 2021.
43 Article 5 is the right to liberty and security of person.
44 App. No. 50086/20.
45 App. No. 50898/20.

Overall, this book has demonstrated the myriad issues which have been raised before the ECtHR regarding state responses to the COVID-19 pandemic. Under the ECHR, states parties had duties to protect the right to life under Article 2 and the right to be free from torture or inhuman or degrading treatment under Article 3 by adopting measures to protect individuals from the virus. However, the difficulty of the issues involved is shown by the fact that the measures adopted, in turn, raised issues regarding their compatibility with rights found in the ECHR. Indeed, as this book has demonstrated, considerably more questions have been raised before the ECtHR regarding the extent to which such measures were compatible with the ECHR than in relation to the extent to which states fulfilled their duties to adopt protective measures in the first place. Nevertheless, it is submitted that the ECtHR must generally be cautious of finding violations of the ECHR in cases involving public restrictions which were applied for the purpose of protecting life and health in response to a global pandemic, as such findings could open the floodgates to a significant number of cases coming before the Court involving similar measures in many other states. Whilst the floodgates argument in itself is not a sufficient reason to hold back from finding a breach of the ECHR, the difficulty is that if the concept of a human rights violation is defined too broadly, it dilutes the seriousness of such a breach. Taken to the extreme, if everything is a human rights violation, then nothing is. In order to preserve the legitimacy of human rights law, the ECtHR must strike the correct balance between holding states to account for clear violations of the ECHR but also being cautious of finding breaches in cases involving public restrictions imposed to protect lives.

Index

For Product Safety Concerns and Information please contact our EU representative GPSR@taylorandfrancis.com
Taylor & Francis Verlag GmbH, Kaufingerstraße 24, 80331 München, Germany

www.ingramcontent.com/pod-product-compliance
Ingram Content Group UK Ltd.
Pitfield, Milton Keynes, MK11 3LW, UK
UKHW022158190926
475702UK00003B/84
9781032468068